西郷（せご）どんと維新の風

敬天愛人の始まり、沖永良部島

Segodon and the Soul of the Meiji Restoration

Bilingual (Japanese/English)

竿田 富夫 著　竿田 豊 訳

日本語／英語2か国版

国書刊行会

西郷（せご）どんと維新の風
――敬天愛人の始まり、沖永良部島

敬　天　愛　人

西郷隆盛座像　昭和62年　東京立体写真像株式会社製作
「穏健にして　憤せず　臆せず　座して正道を求め　天に問う」

【南洲翁遺訓三十】

命もいらず、名もいらず、
官位も金もいらぬ人は、
仕末（しまつ）に困るもの也。
此の仕末（しまつ）に困る人ならでは、
艱難（かんなん）を共にして　国家の
大業は成し得られぬなり。

目次

第二章　生まれ変わった西郷どん　68

第三章　近代日本の夜明け（明治維新）　122

序

世界中の人々から親しまれ愛されている革命的英雄西郷隆盛は、新しい日本の歴史の幕開けとなった明治維新の大偉業を成し遂げ、日本の近代化に貢献しました。

西郷は、この偉業を成す四年前（一八六四年）までは南海の孤島沖永良部島の隔離された狭い牢獄に幽閉されていました。牢生活は想像を絶する程過酷な道のりでしたが、西郷は死をもってその潔白を示すことではなく、生き抜いていくことで真実が明らかとなり、邪を排し正義を守り抜く道であると考えました。それは天が西郷に与えた試練であると悟って座禅を続けます。そして不思議な程西郷自らが生まれ変わっていく自分を見つめることができるようになります。その時の漢詩があります。

獄裡の氷心　苦辛を甘しとし、
辛酸骨に透って　吾が真を看る。
狂言妄語誰か知り得む、
仰いで天に愧ぢず況んや又人にをや。

（解釈）牢獄の中にいると、心は氷のようにまっ白になって、苦さもからさも甘く感じられ、ひどい辛さが骨まで浸み透って自分の本当の心を知ることができる。作り飾った言葉やうそいつわりは誰も見破ることはできない。人を欺くことは易く、天を欺くことはできないものである。自分は天に対して恥ずかしいことはしていないし、まして人に対しても同じである。

牢獄監視役の土持政照は、自分の役目を果たす傍ら、死寸前まで追いつめられた西郷を命をかけて救出します。政照は、西郷の人間としての魅力に惹かれ、何としても助けてやりたい気持ちは、いつも脳裏からはなれませんでした。二人は血を分けた兄弟以上の親密さで結ばれていたのです。敬天愛人の精神はこうした二人の人間愛から自然発生的に芽生えた至上の銘であります。海音寺潮五郎先生は、その著「西郷隆盛」（王道の巻）の中で、沖永良部島の酷遇された牢生活を耐え忍んで生きることが出来たのは、「敬天愛人」の信仰的哲学に達していたればこそである、と述べておられます。

西郷は、一年六か月後に赦免され、希望と勇気を持ち、暖かな南風に乗って日本の大舞台を目ざして飛翔していきます。

第一章においては、正道を守るために生きることに執着する西郷と敬天愛人について述べました。

第二章においては、天を師と仰ぎ、生まれ変わる西郷について述べました。

第三章においては、明治維新などの偉業について述べましたが、成功に導いたのは敬天愛人の精神があったことに注目して読んでいただきたいと思います。

なお、西郷隆盛の偉業については、アメリカ合衆国第三十五代大統領ジョン・F・ケネディをはじめ多くの外国の指導者にも読まれてきたキリスト教徒内村鑑三著『代表的日本人』（英語版）で広く知られているところですが、本書では、南海の孤島で死と隣り合わせの過酷な牢獄生活に喘ぎながらも、それを克服し偉業を成し遂げることが出来たのは、牢獄監視役土持政照や人情味溢れる島民との出会いがあったからこそであり、外国の方々にもこのことを知ってもらいたいために、英訳を付しました。

大変有難いことに西郷隆盛翁の曽孫西郷隆晄（たかみつ）さんから推薦のことばをいただきました。隆晄さんは、平成二十三年八月に初めて来島され親しくお話をしましたが、牢内の曽祖父西郷隆盛翁の座像の前で感激の涙を流されました。現在隆晄さんは、スターライト工業株式会社を経営され、国内外でご活躍の実業家です。また西郷家ご一門のまとめ役としても活動されています。沖永良部島へもその後数回お出でになり親交を深め、西郷南洲記念館建設時には多額のご芳志をいただいております。なお、隆晄様のすばらしい「推薦のことば」からも、曽祖父西郷隆盛翁を読み取っていただきたいと思います。隆晄様に心より感謝申し上げます。

令和三（二〇二一）年二月

著者　竿田　富夫
英訳　竿田　豊

推薦のことば

西郷　隆晄（西郷隆盛の曽孫）

この度、私の尊敬する竿田富夫先生が、「西郷どんと維新の風——敬天愛人の始まり、沖永良部島」を日本文と英文で出版されました。先生は沖永良部島和泊町でお生まれになり、教職の道を進まれ、校長や和泊町教育長をお勤めの傍ら、作曲活動や歴史慈善活動等に多大な功績を残されています。私の印象に深く刻まれているのは、子どもたちへの紙芝居にて、島での西郷南洲翁と島民の触れ合いや歴史を紹介されていたこと、昭和三十九年にヒットした「南国エレジー」（唄高石かつ枝）の作曲者であられたこと、また、西郷家との交わりに於いては、平成二十三年に完成した和泊町西郷南洲記念館建設にご尽力されていたことなどです。これらを通して、私も西郷隆盛の曽孫として百六十数年の時空を超えてのご縁を受け継がせて頂いております。

その一例として西郷家の集いの一つである「二十四日会」（毎年、隆盛の命日である九月二十四日に近い土曜日に百数十人が東京で集う会）に於いても、私から会員の方々に今の沖永良部島と西郷家の〈ご縁〉についての講演をさせて頂き、いつまでもこのご縁が輝きを増していくことを願っている次第です。

さて、私は、早朝起きて散歩をしながら「大自然（天）から生命（いのち）と使命を頂いていることに心から感謝」とつぶやきます。この使命は、西郷隆盛のはるか前の先祖から代々受け継がれており、それぞれがその時代を背負う中で実践して来たのであろうと信じています。その長い永遠の光と重さを感じることが出来る喜びは何にも替えることが出来るものではありません。

曽祖父はあの江戸末期の激動の時代に何かに突き動かされ、どのようなご縁で自身の生命（いのち）を燃やして来たのかが、多くの先生方の書かれた書物や曽祖父の残した書から読み取れます。中でも沖永良部島での出来事は運命とはいえ、過酷な現実でした。そこで改めて自身の使命（天命）に気づき、南国の大自然と人々の温かき心に清められ、蘇り、再生され、いつしか自身の想像を超えた力（エネルギー）となり、現世に戻された様な境遇を走り抜けたのだと思っています。帰還後は思考を超えて、自然な流れで動かされたのだと感じています。

曽孫として私も若い頃は「何故、そこでその判断、行動を？」と分からず、理解し難いことがありました。「どうしてこれだけ多くの若者の命を共に、なぜ？」未だに答えは返って来ませんが、今の私にはいつしか答えは必要でなくなっています。生命を燃やすとはどういうことかと、その一片ぐらいは分かる年齢になったからだと思っています。今は沖永良部島を始めとした曽祖父の足跡の土地でご縁を頂き、共に築いた精神がまだ息づいています。竿田先生にその大きな〈つながり〉を今回の出版を通じて〈はたらき〉として世の中に示して頂きました。有難きことです。心から感謝申し上げます。

私も辛（つら）い時は、沖永良部島で入獄していた曽祖父の銅像を思い浮かべます。そうすると、私ごときの悩みや苦しみは飛んで行ってしまいます。そして曽祖父から「世の為、人の為、隆晄、今、何をしているか？」と問いかけられ「ハッ」と気付かされます。私は、「過去の無限と未来の無限の出会いが今」という言葉が大好きです。この無限への挑戦を竿田先生の出版を通して改めて感じているところです。竿田先生、ありがとうございます。

（スターライト工業株式会社　代表取締役社長）

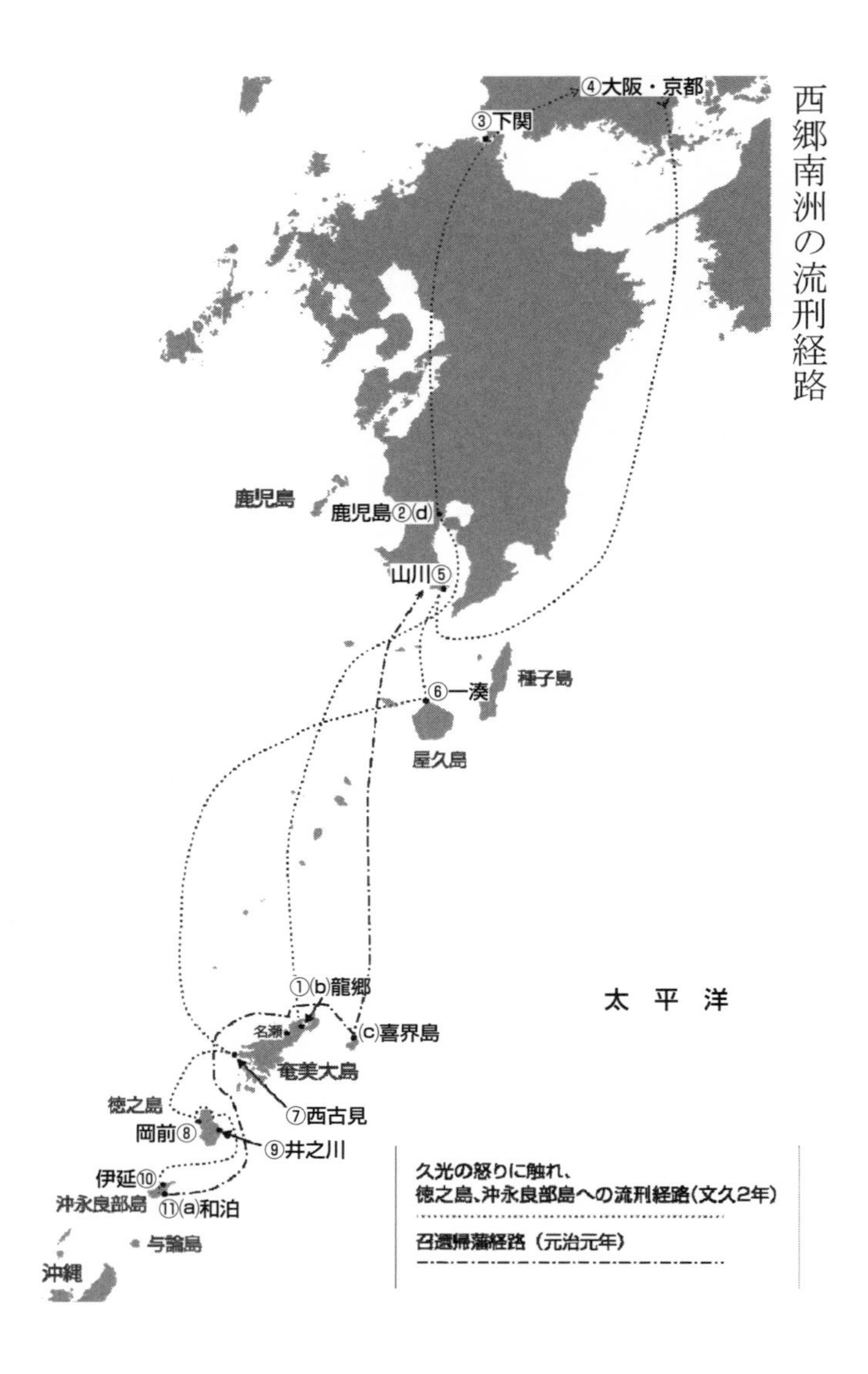
西郷南洲の流刑経路
④大阪・京都
③下関
鹿児島
鹿児島②ⓓ
山川⑤
⑥一湊
種子島
屋久島
太　平　洋
①ⓑ龍郷
名瀬
ⓒ喜界島
奄美大島
⑦西古見
徳之島
岡前⑧
⑨井之川
伊延⑩
沖永良部島
⑪ⓐ和泊
与論島
沖縄
久光の怒りに触れ、
徳之島、沖永良部島への流刑経路（文久2年）
召還帰藩経路（元治元年）

第一章　敬天愛人と沖永良部島

一、西郷どん　徳之島から沖永良部島へ

文久二（一八六二）年閏八月十四日夜が明け東の空が白みかけた。入道雲の切れ目から朝日が顔をのぞかせ、まぶしい。その頃、徳之島井之川港近くの茂った松の木に寄りかかって茫然と空や海を眺めている大男がいました。「愛加那は無事龍郷に帰りついたかな」、「子どもたちは船酔いしなかったかな」などと気にかけていました。愛加那は「この島で

西郷の腰かけ松

親子仲よく暮らせたらなあ」とも言ってくれた。自分のことより妻子のことを思いやる大島吉之助（西郷どん）という男であります。彼は、罪人の汚名を背負ったまま、今日、南の小島・沖永良部島へ再遠島されることになっているその人である。

彼は、この半年の短い間に、苦難の旅を強いられました。国父・久光公の逆鱗に触れたからである。年始には龍郷村にいたが、帰藩の命令により、二月鹿児島、三月下関、四月大坂・京都、五月山川港、七月徳之島、そして閏八月沖永良部島へ遠島となりました。名前もその度ごとに、西郷吉之助、菊池源吾、大島三右衛門、大島吉之助と変名されました。仲間同士では、「吉之助さぁ」「西郷どん」と呼ばれ、奄美では、敬称「西郷先生」でとおっていました。本稿では「西郷どん」、または「西郷」と敬称を省くことにいたします。

さて、話を元に戻しましょう。その日の十時頃になると、井之川の村人たちが西郷を見送りに、港にぞくぞくと集まってきました。中には、「私も連れていって」と涙を流しながら、別れを惜しむ琉仲佑（十六歳）という好少年がいました。少年は、西郷が在島二か月あまり寝食を共にし、身の回りの世話をしながら、学問を教えてもらった師弟の関係にあります。

帆船の護送船報徳丸には、責任者東横目龍の禎用喜と、鹿児島からの警吏（監視員）がすでに乗り込んでいます。

徳之島代官附役の中原万兵衛が西郷に近寄って「出帆後は船牢から出て、自由にお過ごしください、との上村代官からの伝言です。どうぞそのようになさってください」と話しかけておりました。

西郷は、その後みんなに別れの挨拶をして、船牢に入っていかれました。やがて帆船は、井之川港を出港し、順風にのって舵を南へきって走り出しました。しばらくして龍は、「牢を出て自由にしてください」と西郷に出牢をすすめます。西郷は「ありがとう。私は

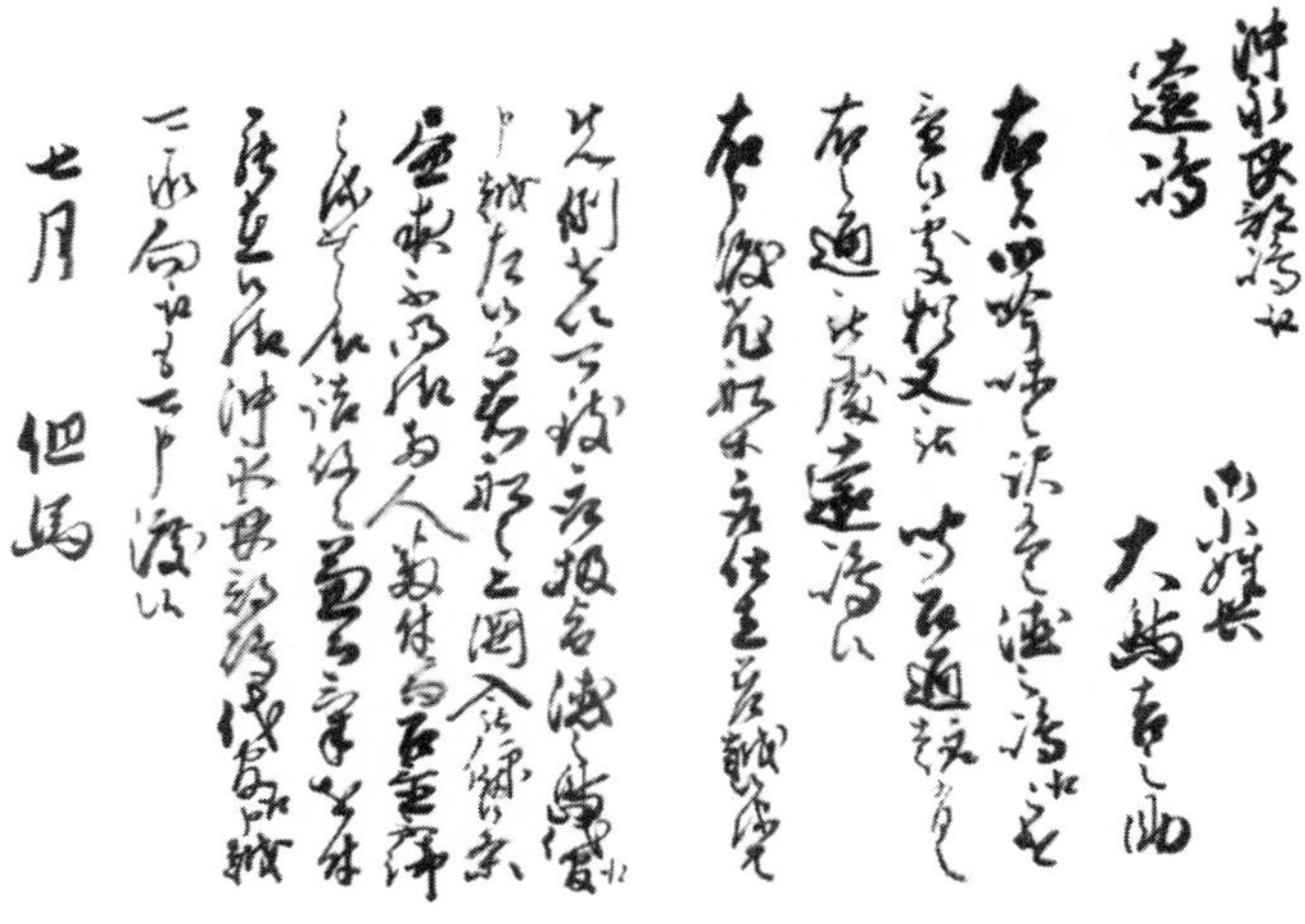

遠島命令書

罪人の身の上ですから、藩命に背くことはできません。気をつかわないでください」と言われ、狭い船牢の中で両足を曲げたままで、書を読んでおられました。西郷の誠実さがしのばれます。帆船は、約四時間要して午後二時頃、沖永良部島の北海岸にある伊延港に着岸いたしました。この港は、沖合いから船着き場まで狭いながらも岩礁がなく、船の出入港に支障はなく、古くから砂糖運搬船や旅客運送に利用されてきております。

　帆船が伊延港に着岸すると、龍は船中に西郷と警吏を残したまま、一里程離れた和泊村にある代官所に急行しました。警吏は、その間に船牢の西郷に一通の手紙を手渡します。それは、大島代官所警衛役の桂久武(かつらひさたけ)からの密書でした。内容は、同志と図って必ず帰藩できるようにするから、決して早まったことをしないように、というものでした。西郷は読み終わってほっとしたのか、一息ついてから笑顔で警吏に声をかけました。

「おまんさあ、見知らぬ顔だが、あたいを海上で殺す刺客とばかり思っておりました。あたいは、あなたの刃がよく刺さるようにと、胸を船べりに寄せておいたのじゃが、当てがはずれたわい、ワッハッハッ」と笑いとばしました。

一方、和泊代官所へ急行した龍は、代官の執務や生活の場となっている大仮屋(おおかりや)に、夕涼みをしていた黒葛原源助(つづらばらげんすけ)を訪ね、命令書を差し出しました。「代官様、大島様の島替(が)えの命令書です。船はもう、伊延港に着いております。」

代官は、突然の出来事にびっくりした様子で、命令書を二、三度読み返し「囲(かこ)い入り仰(おお)せ付けられ候条(そうろうじょう)、昼夜明(あ)けざるよう両人番付(りょうにんばんづ)け、と書いてありますね」。龍は、「上村代官からは、途中、船牢から出して自由にさせよ、と言われ、私もそのようにすすめましたが、大島様は『私は罪人ですから』と牢内にお座りになったままでした。代官様、大島様を早く上陸させてあげてください」と言葉を続けました。

黒葛原代官は、自らの責任の重大さだけを考え、西郷のことなど考える余裕はなさそうです。

「私の一存ではどうにもなりません。お気の毒ですが、そのまま牢ができるまで船中で待っていてください」という返事でした。

龍は、これ以上のことは申し上げる立場にないとあきらめ、代官所を後にして伊延港に引き返しました。

西郷にこのことを話しますと、西郷は「大変ご迷惑をおかけしました。このまま牢にいたほうが気楽で安心です」と言われました。

龍は、護送責任者として、やりきれない気持ちで、西郷と共に船中で一夜を過ごすことにしました。

二、吹きさらしの牢建設

黒葛原代官は、その夜、代官附役や島の役人たちを集め、囲い牢の建設について相談をしました。命令書の牢は、文面からして監視がしやすく牢内がよく見える場所がよいということになり、与人(よひと)役所や番屋にかこまれた狭い土地に決まりました。

翌日、代官は島内から大工を集め、越山（こしやま）あたりの官有林の松材を切り倒し、丸太のまま九尺角の狭い土地の四隅に穴を掘り、これを埋め込み支柱としました。戸や壁の代わりに、少し太めの松材を縦横格子（こうし）式に、間隔をおいてつなぎとめ、床は竹をあら縄であんだものを置き、その上にむしろを四枚重（がさ）ねにしました。厠（かわや）は片すみに穴を掘り、二本の棒を渡しただけのものでした。屋根は薄く茅（かや）をかぶせ、のきを短めに刈り込み、厠は衝立てで仕切り、欠火鉢（かけひばち）のほかは家具はありません。

復元された“吹きさらしの牢”

こうして、お粗末な吹きさらしの牢獄は二日ででき上がりました。

十六日昼過ぎ黒葛原代官は、でき上がった牢の検分を終え、附役の福山清蔵（せいぞう）、間切横目土持政照（つちもちまさてる）を伴って、西郷を出迎えに伊延港に出かけました。

代官は船に近寄り、「代官の黒葛原源助です。牢ができ上りましたので、お迎えにまいりました」と声をかけました。西郷は、着流しの薩摩絣（がすり）にわら草履をはいて船牢の狭い入口をでて、砂浜に下り立ちました。「これはこれは、代官様ですか、大島吉之助でございます。お世話になります」と代官や福山、土持らに挨拶をされました。そして両手を広げて胸いっぱい海の大気を吸われました。

代官は続けて「和泊までは一里程ありますので、馬を用意しました。お乗りください」と乗馬をすすめました。西郷は、「ご厚意はありがたいが、私は罪人です。それに、土を踏むのも最後になるかもしれもはんで、どうか歩かせたもんせ」と乗馬を断り、ゆっくりとした足どりで歩き出しました。

この光景に見入っていた村人たちは、西郷のていねいな言葉づかいや謙虚な態度に心を打たれ、涙ぐむ人もおりました。特に政照は、この時から普通人とは違う人柄に親密感を抱いたようであります。

それから、みんなは西郷の心中を察し、黙々と西郷の後に続きました。

坂道を少し登った所に諸白當(もろはくどう)というお休み処があります。そこで一行は一息入れながら、お茶をもらいました。ふだんは、役を終え薩摩へ帰る役人たちが船待ちに利用する茶店です。

夏の太陽は、昼過ぎでも焼けつく程ぎらぎらと照りつけ、一同は額の汗をふきふき歩き

島津斉彬

続けます。坂道を登りつめたところは、島の尾根に当たり、見晴らしがよく海岸線や洋々たる海が眼下に見えます。太平洋です。西郷は、一瞬立ち止まり、松並木の間から遠くに見える太平洋を見て、今は亡き主君斉彬公の、あの言葉が脳裏に浮かんできました。「今は藩同士で言い争っている時ではない。眼を海外に向け、協力して強い国をつくるべきだ。外国に遅れをとってはならん」と地球儀に手をやりながら、外国の発展ぶりを教えてくれました。今、斉彬公の遺志を果すことができなくなった自分の無力さが悔やまれてなりません。涙が頬を流れ落ちてきました。

道は下り坂になり、家なみには南国特有の風情が感じられます。それぞれの家が、石垣や大木などで囲まれています。空が夕焼けに染まった頃、一行は牢に辿りつきました。代官は、「お迎えのつもりで少々酒肴を用意いたしました。皆さんご一緒にどうぞ」と言いましたが、西郷は「大変ありがたいことですが、咎人は甘えることは許されません、一刻も早く牢へ入れてください」と言われました。龍や警吏は、牢を見て唖然として言葉が出ません。さすがの代官もきまり悪そうに「お粗末でお気の毒ですが」と小さな声をだしました。

西郷はそれ程気にしない様子で「いやぁ、茅の匂い、生木の匂いがよろしいです」と言われ、狭い入口から身をかがめて牢内に入られました。西郷の心遣いや心の広さに政照の尊敬の念は益々深まっていきました。

島津久光

「錠はしっかりかけておいてくれよ。お互いのために安心ですから」と西郷は牢番に声をかけ、むしろの上に座禅を組み、静かに目を閉じられたようです。厳しい牢生活の始まりです。

西郷が、どうして徳之島、沖永良部島へ遠島されることになったかについて、そのいきさつを述べておきましょう。

安政五（一八五八）年江戸幕府は、その安定と存続を図るため、尊皇派の一掃に乗り出し安政の大獄という大事件を起こしました。尊皇派の西郷も幕吏の追手を逃れ、いったん奄美大島・龍郷村に潜居されました。その後幕府の権力は衰えはじめ、外様大名たちの台頭する結果となりました。そして三年後、西郷は帰藩を許され、鹿児島に帰ることができました。

藩主は島津忠義（十六歳）でしたが、若輩のため父久光公が国父という名で藩の実権をにぎっておりました。久光公は帰藩したばかりの西郷に「これから三千名の兵を率いて京都・江戸へ上り、幕政改革を幕府に進言するつもりだ。各藩に通じるお前も同行し、先に出発して下関で情報を収集し、そこで待っていてくれ」と命令しました。

大久保利通（一蔵）

西郷は村田新八を伴い、命令通り下関に到着、そこで聞いた情報はままならない京都の状況でした。それは、久光公が京都に到着しだい、薩摩藩士たちが倒幕に立ち上がるという噂でした。これは久光公の意に反することで、一刻も早く上京して、この動きを思いとどまらせることこそ急務だと考え、大久保一蔵宛て置手紙をして、久光一行を待たず大坂へ向かいました。

一方、三日後に下関に着いた久光公は、命令を無視して上京した西郷らに激怒し、直ちに西郷らを捕縛し、島流しにせよと側近に命じました。心配した大久保一蔵は、西郷の真意を確かめるため一足先に大坂へ向かいました。兵庫の海辺で、二人は、久光公の怒りを鎮めることは困難だと諦めて各々の胸の内を語り合いました。

大久保「島流しになったとしてもいつ帰れるか分からない。あなたを同行させるよう進言した私にも責任がある。いっそのこと二人刺し違えて死のうではないか。」

西郷「死ぬのは俺一人でよか、しかし、今、二人が死んだら尊皇派の同志はどうなるのだ、誰が今の日本を変えるのだ。今は二人とも生き延びて時機を待とう。どうしてもその時宜が来なければ、その時考えればよか。」

西郷は甘んじて島流しの刑を受けることによって、藩が混乱するのを避けたかった。また、盟友大久保一蔵に自ら得た地位を、あえて失わせることはしたくなかったのである。

その翌日、西郷、村田新八、森山新蔵の三名は国元へ帰され、山川港で船中生活をすることになりました。それから一か月半過ぎて、西郷は徳之島へ、村田新八は喜界島へ遠島となりました。森山新蔵は山川港滞船中に自害して果てました。

西郷の徳之島での生活は、主に読書と山登りでした。ある日、琉仲佑少年の案内で山登りに出かけました。山頂あたりに来ますと、西郷は北の方向に見える奄美大島をじっと眺めています。

仲佑「先生、何を眺めておられますか、あの島は徳之島より大きく、人間も多く住んでいます。」

西郷「ああ、そうだね、住んでいる人も多いですね。」

西郷は、近くに見える奄美大島にいる最愛の妻愛加那と子供たちのことに思いを馳せていたのでした。下山の途中、薪を背負った婆さんに出会いました。その婆さんが、西郷に話しかけます。

婆さん「あなた様は二度目の島流しというではないか、私はこの年になるまで二度も島流しにあったという話は聞いたことはありません。昔から二度あることは三度あるといわれます。今度こそ魂を入れかえて立派なおさむらいさんにおなりなさいよ。」

西郷「はい、そのようにします。」

さすがの西郷も、ただ頭をうなだれて聞き入るばかりでしたが、婆さんの悟すような温かい言葉に身が引きしまる思いでいっぱいでした。後でわかったことは、この婆さんの父親も島流しにあったということです。

徳之島遠島二か月後に、愛加那は二人の子供をつれて、奄美大島龍郷村から夫吉之助に会いにやってきました。七か月ぶりの親子の再会に、西郷は、我を忘れる程の喜びかたです。二歳の菊次郎、生まれて四か月の菊子を両手を広げて抱きしめたまま、声が出ません。愛加那は、とめどもなく涙が頬を流れ落ちます。こうした水入らずの喜びも束の間、翌日になると、余りにも非情極まる追加の遠島命令書がとどけられました。その命令書に目を通された西郷は、一瞬全身から力が抜けたようになりましたが、居合わせた人々を見て、

西郷「今度は、もっと南の島に行くことになった。なあに、命だけは助けてあげるということですので、ありがたかことです。」

西郷ならではの気の遣いようです。みんなは慰めの言葉さえみつからずに、ただうつむいたままでした。愛加那は、夫を思いやる心がこみ上げてきて泣きじゃくっています。お上(かみ)の仕打ちにやるせない気持ちでいっぱいでした。

西郷は、兵庫の海辺で大久保と語り合ったことが、現実となったことに信じられないでいます。「その時機が来なければその時に考えればよか。」今が、その時であり、もはや死を覚悟しなければならなかったのです。

その翌日、西郷は同島の井之川村に移され、愛加那は、二人の子供を連れて龍郷村へ帰っていきました。

以上が沖永良部島へ再遠島のいきさつであります。この沖永良部島流罪は、死罪に次ぐ重罪とされています。併わせて家財没収や弟たちの謹慎処分にまでも及ぶことになりました。

三、苦難の道（牢屋ぐらし）

文久二年閏八月（新暦十月初旬）初秋とは言え、焼け付くような陽光が朝から牢内いっぱいに差し込み、西郷は汗をたらたら流しながら座禅、読書そして黙想の日々を過ごされます。逃げ場のない狭い空間の中で長い一日一日が孤独感にさいなまれていきます。

朝夕は、政照が見廻りにきます。彼は、役目を度外視して、最近の出来事や学問のことなど、親密に語りかけ接していきます。西郷は、彼の来訪を唯一の楽しみにしていたようです。食事は、朝のうちに従者の田中窪一（くぼいち）に三食分の麦飯を炊かせておいて、朝は麦飯に僅（わず）かばかりの青菜の入った味噌汁を食べ、昼と夜は冷飯にお湯を流して温め、塩で食べます。間食を断ち、好きな煙草も吸わず、謹慎の誠を尽すことにしていました。

日がたつにつれ、トイレの悪臭はひどく、金蠅が群らがるようになり、昼間はその羽音に悩まされ、夕方になると、やぶ蚊の大群が西郷の体に襲いかかります。

風呂は月一回、牢外に湯桶が準備され入浴が許されます。政照が、風呂上がりに周辺を散歩するようすすめますが、西郷は不謹慎だと言われて、入浴後直ぐ牢へ入られます。

西郷は、どんな逆境におかれても、決して自暴自棄に陥らず冷静な態度を貫き通して、死を覚悟しながらも生死一如の境地を求め、天意天心を識ろうと自己の昇華に努めていきます。

西郷は、何ひとつ悪いことをしていないのに、ひどい処分を受けるようになったが、その特権者に対する憤りがなかったわけではない。その心の憤りを抑えるため、次の二首の漢詩を衝立に大書し、毎日その詩を読み返していました。

読み下し文で書くことにします。

明石藩士　三宅尚斎の獄中作

富貴、寿夭（長命と短命）、心を弐せず

只、面前に向かって精神を養う
四十余年、何事をか学ぶ
笑って獄中に座す鉄石の心

（解釈）社会的地位だとか、名誉だとか、また、長生き、若死にとか、ふたごころを考えず、一直線に前方だけを見つめ、精神鍛練に打ち込み不動の信念を確立する。この四十余年間それのみを学んできたではないか。だから、不動の信念（鉄石の心）を抱いて、こうして心晴やかに獄の中に座っておれるのだ。

森山三十（新蔵）作（西郷、村田と共に山川に戻され、滞船中に自害した。辞世の詩となった。）

慈母悲しむ勿れ　厄に罹るの身
古来此くの如し　幾忠臣
死に臨み　自若として平日の如し
天を怨みず　人を咎めず

（解釈）愛しいお母さん、災いのかかってしまった私を悲しまないでください。昔から
忠義を尽した者はこのようなものです。死を目前にしても、いつもと変わりません。天を怨んだり人を咎めないで、我一人わが信ずる道を行くだけです。

西郷は、この二つの詩を面前にして囲いの中を修業の最適な場所にしようと考えました。それは、若い頃、近くにある誓光寺の無参禅師から大久保らと共に禅を学んだことがあり、再び修養の機会にしようとして座禅を続けることにしました。

この姿を見て、政照は拍子木を持って牢を訪ねました。

政照「ご不自由で大変でしょう。ご用があったらこの拍子木を叩いてください。」

西郷は大変喜んで拍子木を受け取ったが、一度も叩いたことはありませんでした。政照が、「どうして使わなかったのですか」と尋ねると、「別に用がなかったから」ということでした。

また、ある日の夕方、牢を訪ねると、西郷は灯を消して真暗やみの中に座っていました。

「どうして灯をつけないのですか」と尋ねると、

西郷「あっ、政照さん、恥かしい話ですが、夜になって波の音を聞いていると大島の子どもたちのことが思い出されて、つい涙が出てしまいました。人間って弱いものですね。精神を鍛えると言いながら、心の中では、つい過去のことを思い出すものですね。いかん、いかん、あなたをみたら愚痴をこぼしてしまいました。すみません。」

政照は慰めようもなく、「私如きものにもったいないことでございます」と言って頭を下げました。西郷は、牢を後にして帰り行く親切な政照の後姿を、心から拝む気持ちで見送ったのでした。

台風並みに風が強く、雨の日の続くことがありました。そんなある日、夕方になって急に風がビュービュー音を立てて格子戸を通して牢内に吹きつけてきます。近くの小川は海水が逆流して大岩小岩にぶち当たり、飛沫（ひまつ）が斜風（しゃふう）を受けて牢内に入ってきました。西郷は、たまらず衝立てを斜めにして風雨を防ぎ、ぶるぶる震えながら一夜を過ごしました。政照は心配して、あくる日の朝早く牢を訪ねました。

政照「先生、夕べは大雨で大変だったでしょう。」

西郷「政照さんですか、いやぁ、雨も時には風流なものですよ。お陰で昨夜はよい詩ができました。自分でも感心しているところです。これですよ」

と机の上の詩稿を政照に手渡しました。

雨、斜風を帯びて敗紗を叩き、
子規、血に啼き冤を訴えて嘩し。
今宵吟誦す　離騒の賦、
南竄の愁懐百倍加わる。

政照は、詩の意味を尋ねました。

西郷「横なぐりの雨が破れた芭蕉の葉をたたき、ほととぎすは、喉から血を吐くぐらいに無実の罪を訴えてやかましく鳴いている。こんな夜、『離騒』という詩を吟ずれば、南の島に島流しにされたわが身の悲惨さが百倍にもふくれ上がって哀れに思われてならない」

と教えてくれました。西郷は、更に側にあったかごの中から「これも、前に作ったものですよ」と言われて、少し雨に濡れかかった詩稿を見せました。そして、簡潔に意味を教えてくれました。

獄中有感(ごくちゅうかんあり)（七言律詩）

朝(あした)に恩遇(おんぐう)を蒙(こうむ)り　夕(ゆうべ)に焚阬(ふんこう)せらる、
人生の浮沈(ふちん)　晦明(かいめい)に似たり。
縦(たと)い光を回(めぐ)らさざるも　葵(あおい)は日に向う、
若(も)し運開く無きも　意は誠(まこと)を推す。
洛陽(らくよう)の知己(ちき)　皆鬼(みなき)となり、
南嶼(なんしょ)の俘囚(ふしゅう)独り　生を窃(ぬす)む。
生死何ぞ疑わむ　天の附与(ふよ)なるを、
願わくは魂魄(こんぱく)を留(とど)めて　皇城(こうじょう)を護(まも)らむ。

（解釈）　朝方には君公より大事にされながら、夕方には穴の中に生き埋めにされてしまう。人間の運命というものは、空の雲のように定まりのないものだ。葵という花は曇っていても、いつも太陽に向けて咲いている。もし、自分も運が開けず、晴天白日の身になることができなくても、心はいつも忠誠を尽し続けるつもりである。

京都にいた同志たちは皆死んでしまい、南海の孤島に自分一人ぬくぬくと生きているのが不思議なくらいだ。生と死は天の与えるもので、人間の力の及ばぬことは疑いのないことではあるが、願うところは、命がなくなったとしても、魂だけはこの世に留めておいて、天皇をお護りしたいものだ。

＊西郷南洲翁の漢詩は全百九十九首ありますが、最初の漢詩が、この「獄中有感」であります。西郷が獄中で生死のふちをさまよいながらも、いかに天皇をお慕いしていたか、その心中を察することができます。また、江戸城無血開城の二人の英雄、西郷南洲と勝海舟、その勝は自分の家のお墓のそばに、この「獄中有感」の詩を石に刻ませ、「留魂碑（りゅうこんひ）」として建立（こんりゅう）してあります。

西郷は、ひどい粗食（そしょく）や運動不足などのため、体は次第にやせ衰え、声にも力強さがありません。政照は、かねてから栄養のある魚、肉、野菜等母の手料理を女中に言いつけて牢に届けさせますが、西郷は決して箸をつけず、そのまま礼を述べて返すのが常でありました。

政照「先生は、どうして私が届けさせる肴（さかな）や料理を、召し上がってくださらないのですか。」

西郷「お志は十分いただきました。おいしい物を食べた人の死顔はとても見苦しいものだそうです。粗食をした人は晴顔（はれがお）のままといいますからね。」

政照は、西郷の返す言葉を信じられないままでいましたが、かすかに微笑む西郷を見て、さびしさが込み上げてきて、涙が止まりませんでした。

西郷は、藩の不条理な仕打ちにも何の不平も言わず耐え続けています。座禅を組み、書を読み、そして黙想をして、自らの精神鍛錬につとめています。政照は、このような西郷の謹厳な態度や見回りの度に話しかけるやさしい言葉に、人間としての徳の気高さを感じ、そして「投げ打ってでも先生を助けたい」と、そのためなら、自分は、どんな罰を受けようともいとわない気持ちでいっぱいでした。

南洲翁遺訓二十五

人を相手にせず、天を相手にせよ。天を相手にして、己を尽し人を咎めず、我が誠の足らざるを尋ぬべし。

（解釈）人を相手にしないで、いつも天を相手としなさい。天を相手にして自分の誠を尽し、決して人の非を咎めることをせず、自分の真心の足りないことを反省しなさい。

四、土持政照の機転（敬天愛人の極意）

土持政照の生い立ちについて簡単に述べることにします。父親の土持叶之丞（かなえのじょう）綱政（つなまさ）は、薩摩藩士で、天保二（一八三一）年沖永良部島代官所勤務を命じられ来島しました。以後三回に渡って来島し、附役（つけやく）、横目役、そして代官の要職にありました。その間、島育ちのお鶴（つる）と結婚、庶子（しょし）四男（二男は夭逝）をもうけました。長男の政照は四歳になると、父の帰藩に合わせて鹿児島に連れて行かれます。土持本家で厳格な教育を受けながら幼少期を過ごします。十四歳になると、島の母お鶴のもとに帰ることになります。帰島した政照は、その英才を認められ、沖永良部島代官所勤務となります。そして今、西郷と運命的な出会いとなり、西郷の誠実な人柄に心を惹かれ、命をかけて西郷の救出に奮闘努力していくことになります。

秋が深まると、南の沖永良部島にも冷たい北風が吹くようになりました。牢は悪臭がひどくなり、風に乗って周辺にまき散らします。西郷がいかに志が固くとも人間である以上、自然の流れには抗しきれません。髭は顔を覆い、髪はぼうぼうと乱れて赤茶け、頬骨が出っぱって、大きな眼は落ち込み、光がなくなってきました。垢で汚れた体には、袷を重ね着しても骨の髄まで寒さがしみ透ってきます。

暖をとる設備は、政照が持ってきた琉球製の欠火鉢だけで、冷たい風が吹き込むたびに首をすくめながら手をかざします。政照は監視役として、毎日牢を見廻っていて、涙なしでは西郷の姿を見ることができなくなりました。「何とかして助けてあげたい」という自らの役目をも顧みず救出したい気持ちがだんだん強くなってきました。そういうある日の朝方、見廻りに行くとき、ふと遠島命令書に書かれていた「囲入被仰付候条」という文句を思い出し、囲いとは家の中を仕切って造る牢のことに気づきました。それは、西郷が入牢してから三か月が過ぎた頃でした。

吹きさらしの牢と囲い牢の違いに気づいた政照は、これで西郷を救えると考え、すぐさま代官附役の福山清蔵に相談に行きました。かねてから西郷の状態を聞いていた福山も助けたい思いは同じで代官への進言をすすめました。政照は胸を躍らせ大仮屋に黒葛原代官

を訪ねました。政照は息せききって、
政照「代官様、大島様のことでお願いがあります。大島様はこの頃やせ衰えて、まるで幽霊のようです。このままにしておいたら永く持たないと思います。どうか、命令書に書いてある囲い牢に移してください。大島様の今の牢は囲い牢ではなく牢獄でございます。私が人家を買って、その中に囲い牢を作らせますので、どうか、そこに移らせてください。」
代官「お前はよいところに気づいてくれた。全くお前の言う通りだ。家を買うお金はこちらで用意しよう。普請（ふしん）の方はお前に任すから一切取り仕切って早めに造ってくれ。」
政照「代官様、早速お許しくださいましてありがとうございます。普請は私が責任を持っていたします。」
政照はあまりの嬉しさに無我夢中で牢へ飛んで行きました。
政照「先生、先生、代官のお許しがでました。今日限り、この牢を出てください。」
西郷「政照さん、何のことですか、よく分からないのですが。」
政照は、やっと落ち着きを取り戻し、代官への申し入れや代官のお許しのことなど、いきさつをくわしく話しました。語るも涙、聞くも涙、二人とも感極（かんきわ）まって、西郷は格子の間からやせ細った両手を差し出し、政照の肩にしかと抱きつきました。政照も両手をさし延べ、西郷の肩に両手をかけて抱き合い、涙はとめどもなく流れ落ちていきました。

南洲翁遺訓二十四

道は天地自然の物にして、人は之を行うものなれば、天を敬するを目的とす。天は人も我も同一に愛し給うゆえ、我を愛する心を以て人を愛する也。

（解釈）人の踏み行う道というものは、天地おのずからなるもので、人はこれにのっとって行うべきものであるから、何よりも天を敬うことを目的とすべきである。天は人も自分も同じように愛してくれるのだから、自分を大事にする心をもって他人も大事にすることが肝要である。（「敬天愛人」思想）

政照は西郷のぐしゃぐしゃの顔を見て「先生は助かった、命が救われた」と胸が張り裂ける程嬉しかった。そして、天も厳しい試練を乗り越えた西郷に生きていく新しい道を授けたのでした。

人が人に尽すということは、自らを無にすることだと言われるが、政照は己を捨て誠を尽し、今、それが報われようとしているのである。死ぬことよりも生きていくことの苦しさを悟った西郷でしたが、政照の並々ならぬ心遣いに感涙し、何度も目頭をぬぐっております。そして、これからは生きることに執着し、一世の智勇を持って天地に恥じない生き方をしようと心に決めたのでした。敬天愛人の大思想は、このように囲内にて発し、囲外において、その践（せん）をみることになります。

牢番が来て入口の錠を外し、狭い戸が開けられ、西郷は、ふらつきながら格子をつたわって、入口から牢外へ出られました。そして、政照の肩に手をかけ、二人寄り添いながら、三百メートル先の政照宅に辿（たど）り着くことができました。

代官は、政照の西郷を慕う心に感銘（かんめい）を受け、新しい牢造りを許可し、牢が完成するまで身元引受保証人を福山清蔵、住まいを政照宅とし、食事や生活など処遇（しょぐう）の改善を認めることにしました。

十一月初旬、新しい牢の建設が始まりました。敷地は与人役所内の清潔な場所と決まりました。政照は住み心地のよい人家を買い求め、その家の一角を仕切って囲い牢を作り、

土持政照・系図

- フク（皆吉）＝大久保次右衛門 → 利通
- 大久保次右衛門＝チカヒルヤ（徳田） → マツ
- 土持叶之丞綱政＝ツル（豊山） → 政照、政友
- 政照＝マツ → ツル（利安（沖）と結婚）
- 政照＝カネ（町田） → マツ、綱義、綱安、タケ
- 政友＝多嘉（五代） → 政明、綱彦

※綱安＝初代和泊村長
※綱義＝二代和泊村長「流謫の南洲翁」著者

名まえを座敷牢と呼ぶことにしました。工事費は、すべて代官所用の出桝米(でますまい)から下(さ)げ渡すことになりました。出桝米とは大小二個の桝を用意して、島民から上納する米は大桝で、売り渡すときは小桝を使い、そこから生じた剰余米(じょうよまい)を出桝米として代官所用の雑用に充

てていました。

政照は、工事の大工に一日分の仕事を三日かけてゆっくりやるように、と言い含めておいたのでした。できるだけ工事を長引かせて、その間に西郷の健康回復を図ろうと考えてのことでした。

政照宅に起居（ききょ）している西郷は、母お鶴の作る栄養たっぷりの料理をいただき、充分な睡眠、

与人・初代和泊戸長　土持政照

毎日の入浴など家族同様の生活を続け、日増しに体力をつけ、健康を取り戻していきました。西郷は腕まくりをして「こんなに肥りました。政照さん、お母さん、マツさん、ありがとう」と礼を述べます。政照親子も西郷の嬉しそうな様子を見るのが楽しみでした。夜になると政照と両人で晩酌をするのが楽しみのひとつでありました。時折、附役の福山、高田もやってきて座がにぎわいます。酔がまわると西郷は、「今晩は江戸仕込み（じこ）の箱入りじゃ」と言って、大声で唄を歌いはじめます。政照は西郷の唄となるとハラハラさせられます。代官の住む大仮屋とは二丁（ちょう）程しか離れていないからです。余りに興が過ぎると西

郷に科(とが)がかかるのを怖(おそ)れたからであります。

政照「先生、もっと優しい声で歌ってください。それでは、唄になりません。」

西郷「ハハ……。黒葛原殿への気兼ねじゃな。なに、ここは牢でなか(ないので)で、唄を歌って悪いという法はないが、その時はなー、福山どん、おはんが俺の引き受け人じゃって、代わって牢に入ってくいやんせ。」

一同は、互いに見合って高笑いで、座はなお愉快なものになっていきました。

政照は西郷の晴々とした笑顔を見て、ほのぼのとした気分でいっぱいになりました。

五、座敷牢の日々

座敷牢は、二十日余りかかって漸(ようや)く出来上がり、西郷は政照宅からここに移り住むことになりました。座敷牢は、二間半角(けんはんかく)の家の中に九尺四方の広さで、通風採光ともによく床下も高く、厠(かわや)、湯殿(ゆどの)も付設され衛生的なものになりました。
西郷「政照さん、おはん(あなた)のお陰で、よか隠居部屋(いんきょべや)が出来ました。遠島人には贅沢(ぜいたく)すぎます。」

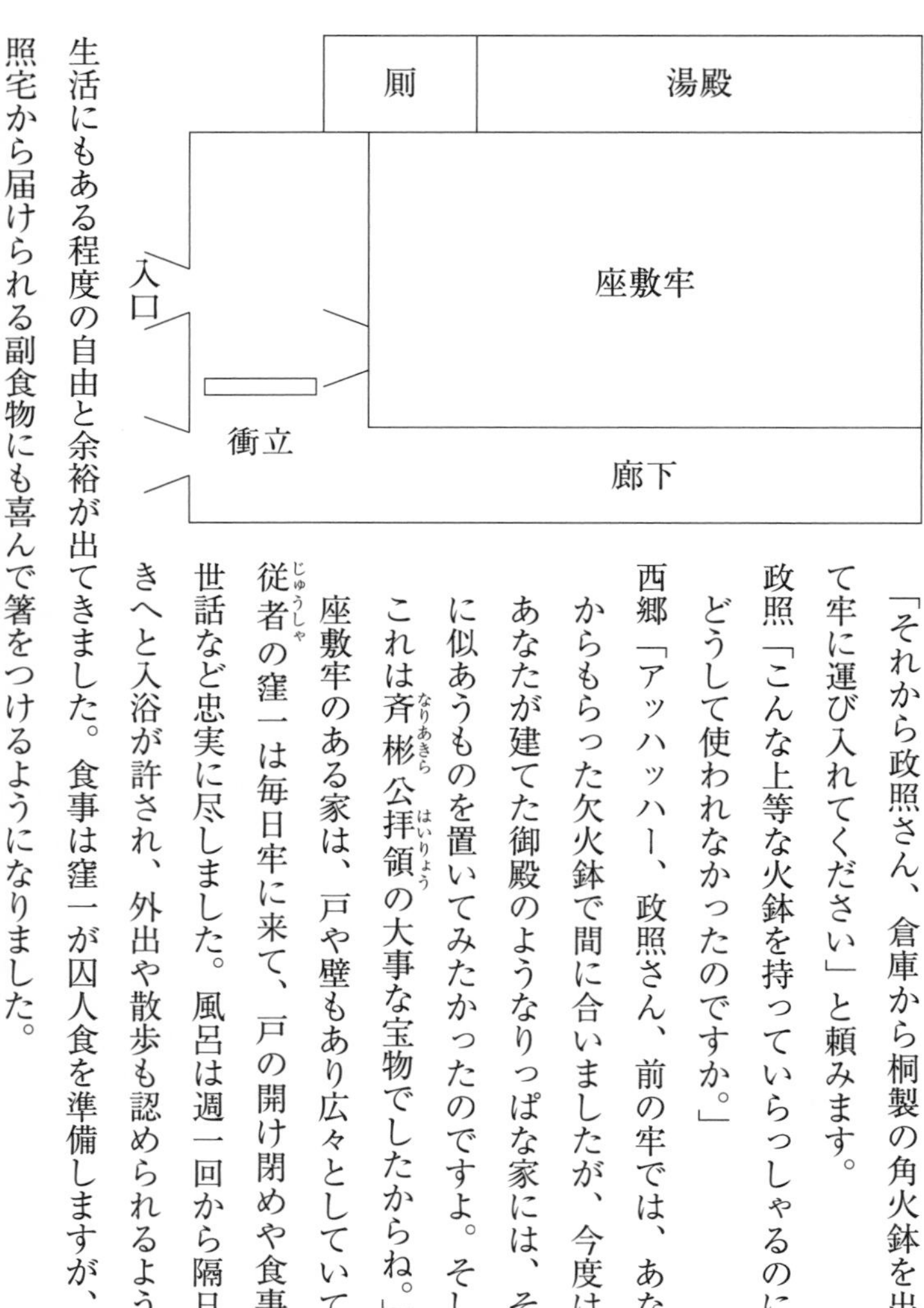

「それから政照さん、倉庫から桐製の角火鉢を出して牢に運び入れてください」と頼みます。

政照「こんな上等な火鉢を持っていらっしゃるのに、どうして使われなかったのですか。」

西郷「アッハッハー、政照さん、前の牢では、あなたからもらった欠火鉢で間に合いましたが、今度は、あなたが建てた御殿のようなりっぱな家には、それに似あうものを置いてみたかったのですよ。そして、これは斉彬(なりあきら)公拝領(はいりょう)の大事な宝物でしたからね。」

座敷牢のある家は、戸や壁もあり広々としていて、従者(じゅうしゃ)の窪一は毎日牢に来て、戸の開け閉めや食事の世話など忠実に尽しました。風呂は週一回から隔日おきへと入浴が許され、外出や散歩も認められるように、生活にもある程度の自由と余裕が出てきました。食事は窪一が囚人食を準備しますが、政照宅から届けられる副食物にも喜んで箸をつけるようになりました。

西郷は、座敷牢に移ってから住環境など改善はみられましたが、決して甘えることはありませんでした。命令にそむかず、運命を逃げませんでした。夜空に冴(さ)える月を眺めながら前の牢のことが頭をかすめます。昼とも夜ともわからない夢うつつの中で過ごした幾日間を思い出し、今生きているのが不思議なくらいでありました。あの逆境にあえぐ自分を、政照は自らの職務を顧(かえり)みず、命をかけて代官に直訴(じきそ)し、救出してくれました。「我を愛する心をもって人を愛する。」これが、天地自然の道（天の心）である。と、窓から差し込む月あかりに照らされながら、政照親子へ手を合わせ感謝の心でいっぱいでした。これからは、生まれ変わって、生きられるだけ生きのびて、少しなりとも政照親子への恩返しや島の人々のために役立とうと決心したのでした。

六、座敷牢における読書

西郷の読書熱は、若い頃の下加治屋町の郷中(ごじゅう)教育に端を発します。「りっぱな武士になりたい」の一心から人一倍勉学に励み、刀傷を負ってからは武芸をあきらめ、一層文芸、特に読書に精を出したようであります。二才頭(にせがしら)を務めたときは、誓光寺(せいこうじ)に通い無参禅師(むさんぜんし)

から禅を学び、江戸詰めのときは藤田東湖などの薫陶を受けています。沖永良部島へ遠島のときは千二百冊余りの和漢の書を三つの行李に入れて持参してきています。西郷は、座敷牢を最適な読書の場と決め、朝から晩遅くまで没頭するようになりました。

西郷が読んだ主な書をあげてみると、

○和　言志四録（佐藤一斎）　嚶鳴館遺草（細井平洲）

○漢　論語（孔子）　孟子　大学　中庸（四書）

易経　書経　詩経　礼記　春秋（五経）

近思録　韓非子　荘子　陳龍川文鈔　孫子

王陽明鈔録　古文真宝　通鑑綱目

○操家から借りて読んだ書

唐詩選　文選　九成宮醴泉銘

内容一部の例

○言志後録三十三条

「春風を以て人に接し　秋霜を以て自らを慎しむ」

（人に対しては春風のように暖かく接し、自分に対しては厳しくせよ。）

○言志後録六十四条
「晦に拠る者は能く顕を見、顕に拠る者は晦を見ず」

（暗い所にいる者は、明るい所にいる者をよく見ることができるが、明るい所にいる者は、暗い所にいる者の気持ちを解ることができない。……弱い立場の人々の声をよく聞け。）

○言志晩録七十条
「われはまさに、人の長処を視るべし、人の短処を視ることなかれ、短処を視れば、即ち、われ彼に勝り、われにおいて益なし、長処を視れば、即ち、彼われに勝り、われにおいて益あり」

（人と接するときは、その人のよい所だけを見つけてほめてやれば、結局は、自分にとってプラスになる。……謙虚であれ、と。）

○論語
　子曰　己の欲せざる処人に施す勿れ。
　子曰　学びて思わざれば、即ち罔し、思いて学ばざれば、即ち殆し。

子曰　過ちて改めざる、是を過ちと謂う。

○陳龍川文鈔

「一世の知勇を推倒し　萬古の心胸を開拓す」

（ありったけの知識と勇気を駆使して、未来永劫に残る心と体を切り開く）

＊西郷は、自ら建設した吉野開墾社の入口に、この漢詩を揚げ、皆の志気を高めた。

○嚶鳴館遺草（細井平洲）

巻第二（政の大体）人は四季の移ろいの中に生きている。春暖に種を植え、夏暑に成長させ、秋涼の中に実り、冬寒に収穫となる。天地の大きな徳を受けながら働き、生活をしている。政を進める上で、自然に目を向け、公平の大切さを知るべきだ。

＊米沢藩が大飢饉だった時、藩主上杉鷹山は細井平洲を招き、政・経・教等改革を行い、藩を立て直した。その民政の根本となった、この本を鷹山に献上した。

＊西郷は、好んでこの本を読み、川口雪篷と二人で全六巻を筆写し、政照に与えた。与人役大体、横目役大体、社倉趣意書の内容にも生かされている。

西郷は、持参した本のほかに、操家の蔵書を借りて読んでいます。その場合必ず借用書を書くようにしています。

西郷先生の礼儀正しい人柄があらわれています。

（例）

今日も御嘉祥奉賀候　然らば古文二冊卒度拝借御願申上候　些見合度儀御座候間此段得御意候

頓首

十二月五日

吉之助

坦勁（たんけい）様

（意）ご機嫌いかがでしょうか、古文二冊をちょっとお貸しください。すこしばかり調べてみたいものがありますので、よろしくお願いします。

七、西郷塾とその弟子たち

座敷牢での生活は、読書が中心となり、体の一部とも言われる程、本と向き合っていました。政照は、端座して読書する西郷の姿を見て、好意を寄せ尊敬の念を一層強く持つようになりました。そして「先生、和泊の子どもたちに学問を教えてください。子どもたちも、本読みを習いたいようです」。西郷は、政照の頼みを喜んで受け入れ、子どもたちを集めるように指示しました。

和泊村の操坦勁、市来惟信、鎌田宗圓、手々知名村の矢野忠正、沖利経ら十五、六歳の少年が希望して弟子入りしました。西郷は、かつての郷中教育のことを思い出し、個別指導や集団指導を効果的に取り入れ、懇切丁寧に教えてやりました。朝から昼までは素読、夜は講釈を基本としました。西郷は、囲いの中に居て書を講じ、子どもたちは囲いの外の廊下に正座して、これを聴聞するという特異な塾でありました。離島僻地の恵まれない青年たちを一人前に育て上げてやろうとする西郷の熱意の発露であります。

西郷塾で教えた主なものは、四書五経、近思録、言志録、嚶鳴館遺草などで、人生、道徳、政治、学問に関する内容が多く、子どもたちは、偉大なる西郷の教えを実践窮行、率先垂範という風でありました。

また、この子どもたちは、座見廻りとして代官や役人の仮屋等に数日間給仕役として勤めています。これは、役人になるための「行儀見習い」の名目での実地研修であり、「仮屋の坊」と呼ばれていました。西郷塾では「仮屋の坊」学習も重視し、役人の初歩の段階として、挨拶、言葉遣い、礼儀作法などを身につけさせ、生きて働く教育を目指していたのでありました。

西郷塾は、年が明けて町田順圓、沖緝賢らが次々と弟子入りし、総数二十名程となりました。西郷が、鹿児島の叔父椎原兄弟に送った手紙の中に次のようなことが書かれています。

「書物読み弟子二十名計に相成り、至極繁栄にて鳥なき里の蝙蝠と申す儀にて、朝から昼までは素読、夜は講釈共仕りて、学者の塩梅にて独笑しく御座候。然し乍ら学問は獄中のお陰にて上り申候。御一笑成し下さるべく候。」

わずか一年余りの間の西郷塾ではありましたが、その影響は大きく、西郷帰藩後も、その学習熱は弟子たちに受け継がれ、孫弟子、曽孫弟子に広がり、沖永良部島発展の基盤となっています。

○西郷塾の学問の例

・論語、孟子の教え―五倫五常（人の常に守るべき道徳）

五倫―君臣の義　父子の親（しん）　夫婦の別　長幼の序　朋友の信

五常　仁　義　礼　智　信

・大学「明徳とは、汚い欲に覆われていない赤心の表れ、天の心。新民とは、民を励ますこと、上役に汚い政治をさせぬこと。至善（しぜん）とは、よい政治をして、世人を安心させること。」

・孟子「人はもともと生まれるということを知って生まれてきたものではない。だから、いつ死ぬかも知りようがない。時が来たら、天から授かりしままでお返しすればよい。

（生死一如）

ある日の朝、西郷は牢の掃除にきた操坦勁少年に、「坦勁さん、あなたは余程学問が好きなようじゃが、一家が睦まじくするには、どうすればよいと思いますか」と尋ねました。坦勁は、教えられた言葉の中から、「それは五倫五常（ごりんごじょう）の道を行うことにあります」と即座に答えました。「アッハッハー、よく覚えていますね。」西郷は、今こそ生きた学問を教えるよい機会と捉えて、机上の紙に次のように書いて坦勁に渡しました。
「此説キ様ハ、只当リ前ノ看板ノミニテ今日ノ用ニ益ナク、怠惰ニ落チ易シ　早速手ヲ下スニハ欲ヲ離ルル処其第一ナリ　一ツノ美味アレバ一家挙テ共ニシ衣服ヲ製ルニモ必ズ善キハ長ニ譲リ、自分勝手ヲ構ヘズ互ニ誠ヲ尽スベシ　只欲ノ一字ヨリ親戚ノ親ミモ離ルルモノナレバ根拠スル処ヲ断ツガ専要ナリ　サスレバ慈愛自然ニ離レヌナリ」

西郷は、書いた紙を渡してから、具体的に教えました。「五倫五常も、最もなことだが、その言葉に固守してしまうと中途半端になってしまう。よい方法は、欲を出さないことが第一である。おいしい物は家族みんなで分け合い、着物は年上から順に作って互いに誠を尽すことが大切である。欲の一字のために、親子、親戚の親しみも離れるものであるから、不和のもととなる欲を断ち切れば慈愛の心は永久に離れないものである」と。

沖永良部島には、西郷塾のほか遠島人の塾、島の学者の開いた塾など三十か所余りの私塾があり、学習環境は、ほかのどの島よりも恵まれ、役人、医師、教員、弁護士等を輩出し、進取の気性に富む風土が生まれていました。

○和泊村の塾

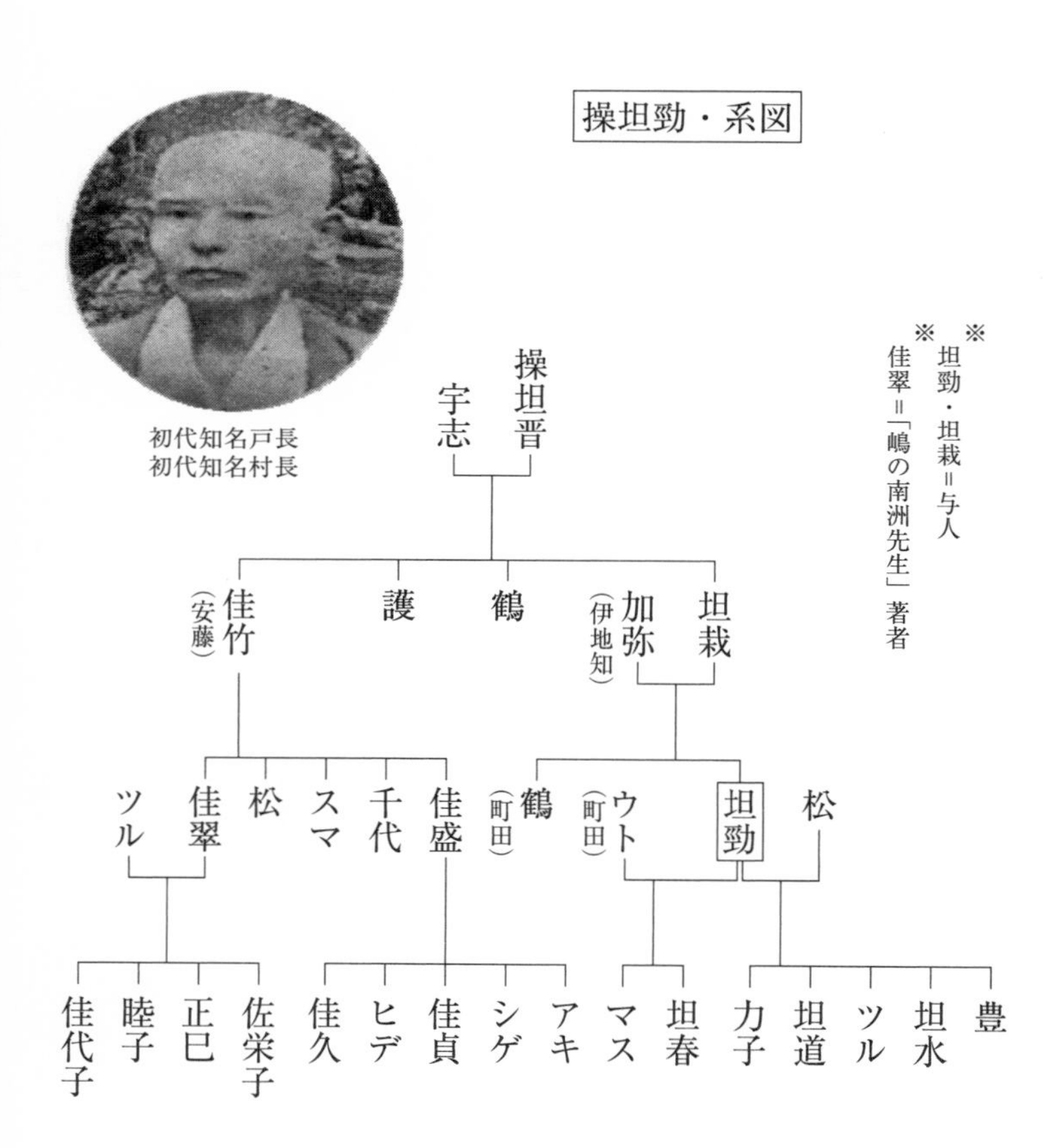
操坦勁・系図
初代知名戸長
初代知名村長
※坦勁・坦栽＝与人
※佳翠＝「嶋の南洲先生」著者
操坦晋
宇志
坦栽
加弥（伊地知）
鶴
護
佳竹（安藤）
松
坦勁
ウト（町田）
鶴（町田）
佳盛
千代
スマ
松
佳翠
ツル
豊
坦水
ツル
坦道
力子
坦春
マス
アキ
シゲ
佳貞
ヒデ
佳久
佐栄子
正巳
睦子
佳代子

竹夏鼎幹　操坦晋　沖島曽勲　栄寿鳳　撰玄碩
安藤佳竹　鎌田宗圓
○手々知名村の塾
町右左則　沖蘇廷良　龍真玉橋　玉江福村　矢野忠正
○内城村の塾
宗平安隆　豊山真粋敏　甲文郁
○余多村の塾
安田蘇泉　今栄民直　中村宮久二
○遠島人の塾
和　紀平右衛門
田皆　新納平太夫
瀬利覚　染川四郎左衛門
余多　平瀬市助
上城　小田善兵衛
内城　曽木藤太郎

西原　川口雪篷
喜美留　児玉萬兵衛
黒貫　村田
国頭　市田忠太郎
皆川　平富里　竹之内助市
玉城　五郎左衛門

明治時代になると学校制度ができ上り、地域では塾の時代から、集落ごとの勉強会へと衣替えしていきます。吾館(あかたじ)学友会、和泊後進舎(こうしんしゃ)、そして、新進舎、夜学校と地域ぐるみで青少年教育を支えていきます。

沖永良部島の遠島人は、重罪人とされているが、流刑に処せられたとはいえ、普通の罪人とは異なり、ほとんどが政治犯や学者であり、学徳の秀れた者たちでした。沖永良部島の教育文化、政治、経済、暮らしなど発展の基盤は西郷はじめ遠島人によって築かれたといっても過言ではありません。

八、年明けて

沖永良部島にも文久三（癸亥）年の正月がきました。西郷は、亥の年生まれで、この年、数え三十七歳の年男です。牢にも、新年を祝って豚肉が一斤、二斤と届けられてきました。政照母子は、僅かに心尽しの酒肴を携えて牢を訪ねました。囲いの内と外を隔てて祝杯をあげました。

この年の三月、黒葛原代官らは二年の任期を終え、鹿児島に帰ることになりました。福山と高田は旧知の間柄であり、辞去には互いに心残りがありました。高田は、西郷が鹿児島に帰られる時、丸腰では大変困ることだろうからと、短刀一振りを差し上げるようにと、福山にあずけておいてありました。後に西郷は、高田にお礼の手紙と感謝の詩を贈っています。

（詰役）	文久元年、二年	文久三年、元治元年
	代官　黒葛原源助	代官　山田平蔵
	附役　福山清蔵	付役　木藤源左衛門

三木原甚左衛門　　川口萬次郎
赤崎源助
横目　高田平次郎　　横目　鎌田八之丞
山口七之助

新任の山田代官は、牢に西郷を訪ね、着任の挨拶をいたしました。一応の儀礼的な言葉を交わした後、次のようなやりとりがありました。

山田「中山様からも、特によろしく申し上げてくれと言うことでした。そして、気をつけてお世話するように言われました。」

西郷「あなた代官でしょう。代官はうそを言ってはいけません。中山殿が俺のことを頼んだりするはずがない。」

西郷は怒気（どき）を含めて言い返しますが、山田は万事を尽して伝言を伝えようとします。側で聞いていた政照は、又もや、これがために西郷の取り扱いが悪くならないかと心配でなりません。

なる程、西郷の流謫（るたく）の因（もと）は、中山尚之助（しょうのすけ）らの讒言（ざんげん）から始まったことであり、代官の中山伝言は空々しく聞こえたものでした。しかし、その後の中山は、西郷の論が正しく、自分の間違いだったのに気づき、西郷の赦免に努力したということでありました。西郷には、このことは、知る由もなかったわけです。

九、西郷どんと川口雪篷（せっぽう）

西原（にしばる）村に川口雪篷・香雲（こううん）（量次郎（かずじろう））が、遠島人として住んでいました。彼がこの島に流されたのは嘉永四年で、早十年が過ぎようとしています。先祖は種子島でしたが、彼は江戸生まれで江戸育ちであります。若い頃、陽明学を修め、書道の達人であり、詩作にも通じています。久光公の写字生として鹿児島に住んでいましたが、父兄の不始末で、連座（れんざ）制によりこの島に流されたのでした。西原村では塾を開き多くの門弟を輩出しています。東一元、西村、柏、池田など医師、教師として活躍しています。

雪篷は当時四十六歳、西郷より九歳先輩に当たります。西郷の帰藩後間もなく鹿児島に帰されましたが、一時娘婿のもとに身を寄せました。その後、西郷家の食客となりながら私学校の教師となり、西郷の戦死後、西郷家を守り、明治二十三年、七十三歳で病死しました。鹿児島市浄光寺にある「西郷隆盛墓」「村田新八墓」の墓碑の字は雪篷の書であります。

雪篷は見廻り役の政照に頼んで西郷を牢に訪ねました。初対面のときから西郷の人間味の温かさ、謙虚さ、そして、誠実さなどの人柄に心を惹かれ、また、西郷は名利(みょうり)にとらわれず、何事にもこだわらない明るい性格の雪篷に惚(ほ)れ、親交を重ねていきました。

雪篷は酒好きで、時折とっくりをぶらさげて牢にやってきます。飲んでは歴史についてディスカッションをし、国家盛衰論を語ったり、書や詩の手ほどきをしたりして、時のたつのも忘れて語り合いました。「牢屋者はいいな、働かずして飯にありつける」などと冗談を言って笑いとばす、雪篷は話し疲れると、そのまま牢の廊下にいびきをかいて寝込んでしまうことも一度や二度ではありませんでした。西郷は、「あなたは睡眠先生と呼んだほうがよく似合う」とからかうと、「いや、酔う酔眠先生でよか」と談笑は尽きません。

また、ある日の朝早く西原村を出たものの、道に迷い、仕方なく野原で休んでいると、幸い草刈りの農夫が通りかかりました。道を教えてもらい、夕方になってようやく牢に辿りつきました。話を聞いた西郷は、「昼日中狐に化かされた話はきいたことがない。あなたはうっかりしていたんでしょう。今日からは酔眠先生をやめて『迂闊(うかつ)先生』と呼ぶことにしよう」「どうでも勝手に、名前はいくらでも多い方がよい」。二人とも、話に花を咲かせ笑いころげました。

現今、西郷の書を見ると、雪篷の書風の影響を受けていたことが明らかにわかります。また、西郷の詩は、ほとんどが沖永良部島以後のものであり、雪篷の手ほどきを受けてから本格的になったこともうなずけるところであります。

第二章

生まれ変わった西郷どん

一、天を師と仰ぎ生まれ変わる

文久三年の正月もやっと過ぎ、春先の暖かさが感じられる季節となってきました。雨の日が続いたためか牢近くを流れる小川の水かさが増し岸辺には蛙がたむろして、やかましく鳴き声を上げている。島の人々は農事に多忙を極め、朝早起きして畑に出かけ、唐芋の植え付け、砂糖きびや麦の中耕など夜遅くまで仕事に余念がないと政照は西郷に話していました。

西郷は農業の話を聞いて、幼少のころ父親に急かされ、大根畑に連れて行かれて鍬作業を手伝わされたことを思い出しています。「お前は長男、下級武士の給料だけでは弟、妹の面倒は見られない、農業を続けなければならない」と悟された。そのつもりだったのが、藩主斉彬様お側近くに仕えることになり、京都、江戸での藩の仕事が多くなってきました。英明篤実な斉彬様は、西郷を自らの片腕とし、仕事を教える傍ら外国の情勢についても説き、日本の進む道を教示するようになりました。また、斉彬様は越前の松平春嶽に「私には多くの家来がいるが、いざというとき役に立つ者は西郷吉之助という者一人だけだ。しかし、彼は独立心が強く私でなければ使うことができない」と話されたことを盟友橋本左内殿から聞かされた。君主と家臣は堅い絆で結ばれていたのです。西郷は、斉彬様の訃報に接した時、殉死できなかったことを今更ながら悔やんでいるようです。西郷にとって斉彬様は主人であり、人生の師でもありました。沖永良部島へ遠島になってからは、危うく牢死するところを政照に助けられ、その後、天を後半生の師と仰ぎ、生きられるだけ生きることに執着し、敬天愛人を至上の銘として生まれ変わっていったのです。「すべては天が自分に与えた道だから」と、天命を悟っていました。

いつしか従者の窪一が廊下の戸を開けてくれていた。牢内に朝日が差し込み、さわやかな春風が心地よく吹き通っていった。以前の牢とは比べようもないほど快適な座敷牢でした。西郷は時折、背伸びして深呼吸をしたり手足を動かしたりして、牢が狭く感じられるように思われてきました。政照の母お鶴さんが牢に届ける滋味ある食も喜んで箸をつけ、体も太り体力も増してきたように政照には思われました。

西郷が明るく振舞い、精神的にポジティブになったことが政照には何よりも嬉しかった。講談を演じたり雪篷や牢を訪ねる人々と談笑したり好きな相撲で島内を沸かせたりして、普通人と変わらぬ特異な囚人でありました。

二、「牢屋の先生」相撲を取る

座敷牢に移ってから住環境は改善され、食事や運動などの待遇もよくなりました。地域の人たちとの交際も楽しく、精神的にも安定してきて体力も、以前の西郷に戻りつつあります。

「政照さん、お陰で元気になりました。何のお礼もできませんが、相撲を取って元気なところを見てもらいたいのですが、相手を探してくださいませんか。」

政照は、西郷の相撲取りは以前に聞かされていたので、楽しみに相手を探しました。松尾璞潤（ぼくじゅん）という島きっての相撲取りを連れてきました。早速、牢前の広場（砂浜）に、俄（にわか）土俵が造られました。勝負は三回取って二回勝つと勝ち名乗りを受けられます。多勢の見物人に囲まれて二人とも緊張ぎみです。相撲巧者の西郷が二回続けて勝ち、勝ち名乗りを受けました。人々の間から盛んな拍手が沸き起こりました。このことは情報網のない島でも、その日のうちに「相撲取りの西郷先生」として、島中のニュースになりました。人々の間では「牢屋の先生」と呼び、西郷を身近な友人として親しみを持って、こう呼んだのでした。素朴で純粋、今を生きる人々にとって西郷はいつしか、愛称「牢屋の先生」として広く尊敬されていきました。西郷は、ほかに相撲取りはいないかと政照に聞きました。政照はその三日後に附役川口萬次郎の飯炊きをしている三五郎を連れてきました。彼は巨体で筋骨たくましく、場所も踏んでおり、相手なしと威張っておりました。三五郎は、「力が違い過ぎると、大怪我をすることもあるので」と始まる前から自信満々です。観衆は垣を作るほどのにぎわいになり、「牢屋の先生、きばれ」の大コールが沸き、両人とも秘術を尽して烈しくぶつかり合います。これも西郷の技がまさり、物の見事に土俵中央に投げつけました。二回とも西郷が勝ち、勝ち名乗りを受けました。西郷は「牢屋の先生」のニックネームで島のヒーローになりました。

政照は、西郷の体力回復を喜び、「誠を尽す」ことの大事さを教えられた気持ちになり、涙が出るほど嬉しくなりました。

三、講談と扇子(せんす)

西郷はこのところ、牢に居ても平和で恵まれていることに感謝しているように思われます。政照の毎日の見廻り、木藤は牢に来て天下の情勢を語り、雪篷の詩・書の手ほどきも面白くなってきました。二十名の弟子たちからは、「先生、先生」と衷心から慕われ、また、与論島詰役の川口萬次郎、沖縄の米良(めら)助右衛門からも面白い通信が送られてきます。人の情程有難いものはないと、ますます幸せを感じるようになりました。

そんなある日、政照は仕事を終え、酒肴を持って牢を訪ねました。西郷の話や笑顔を見聞するのが楽しみになっていたのでした。西郷は、杯を重ね、快く酔が廻ってくると、いつものように、「今日は軍談を聞かせよう。扇子を貸してくれ」と言って、政照が持ってきた扇子を借り、煙草盆をひっくり返して、その底を叩きながら「宮本武蔵」や「曽我兄弟物語」を面白くおかしく語ります。

政照は聞き終わると、「先生、実に愉快でした。話は一流ですが、扇子が叩き破られて使い物になりません。もう、五、六本損じましたよ。ひとつ、弁償してもらいましょうかな」とからかいます。西郷は、にこにこしながら、「私の軍談はたくさん資本がかかっております。それを、お金も出さずに、ただで聞いて、扇子代を弁償してくれとは、余りに欲が深すぎませんか」二人は腹を抱えて大笑いしました。

四、牢で烏賊（いか）を釣る

西郷は、従者窪一に臭木（くさぎ）（カバシニャ）の老木を見つけて、その根っこの節くれだったところを切って、四、五本持って来てくれと頼みました。奄美大島・龍郷にいたとき、烏賊餌木（えぎ）の造り方を習った西郷は、二、三日、余念なくその臭木を削り、見事な烏賊餌木を五、六本造りました。そこに、徳之島で知り合った船員がぶらりとやってきて、「先生、私が大烏賊を釣って差し上げますので、餌木を一晩だけ貸してください」と言ったので、手ごろな物を持たせてやりました。二日後に大烏賊二匹が牢に届けられたので、政照宅に持って行かせました。政照は不思議に思って、西郷に聞いてみると、西郷は笑いながら、「どうです、政照さん、大名人ともなれば、囲いの中でも大烏賊が釣れるでしょうが、これからも釣ってあげますから、楽しみに待っていてください」とにこやかに笑いました。が、西郷は大烏賊を届けにきた漁師風の男に、大烏賊はありがたくもらいましたが、餌木はどうしましたかと尋ねると、「あの人は牢屋の中にいるので、追っかけて来られない」と言って、徳之島へ持ち逃げしたと言われました。西郷はあきれ顔で、言葉が続かなかったようです。

五、「南洲」雅号(がごう)

文久三年初秋の頃、与人蘇廷良(そていりょう)(貞卿)から茄子(なす)が牢に届けられました。見るからに色よし、香りよし、味よしの三拍子揃った見事な料理でした。調理は政照の母お鶴のお手製のもの。その上、料理に添えられた和歌が、最も喜ばしく心を惹かれました。西郷は、お礼に次の漢詩を贈って感謝の意を表しました。

貞卿先醒の茄を恵まれしを謝す
麗色の秋茄　一段の奇、
依然たる芳味　君に依って知る。
正に厚情の深き処を見るを要す、
添賜の佳声　最も悦嬉す。

南洲拝

（解釈）　色の美しい秋茄子が格別に珍しく、昔に変わらぬ芳しくおいしい味を君の恩恵によって賞味することが出来て誠に有難いが、君の厚い情の最も深くこもっている点はどこにあるかを知らねばならない。見事な茄子に添えて賜った美しい歌が最も喜ばしくて嬉しい。

＊　西郷が雅号「南洲」を使用したのは、この詩が最初であります。南の嶋を意味しており、自らの雅号としたのであります。
「貞卿」は蘇廷良の雅号であります。

六、政治の根本を教える

西郷は、命の恩人政照が将来この島を背負って立つ与人等の役職につくことを見抜いて、そのための心得をまとめ、与人役大体、横目役大体として書き与えています。内容は、現実的、具体的なものであり、現職にある役人らも実行に備えたと言われます。要旨をまとめてみました。

(一) 与人役大体

1、役人というものは、島民の生命、財産を預かる最も大事な職である。若し与人一人が誤った事をすれば、数千人数万人の人民を誤まらせることになるので小さな事でも慎重に考え、大事に実行しなければならない。

2、一番大事なことは、人民の信頼を得ることである。何事も自分の思いのままに動かすことが出来るなどと考えたら、すぐ信頼を失い、万人の仇敵となってしまうから慎重に行動することが肝要である。

3、常に人民の悩み苦しみを自分の悩み苦しみと考え、また、人民の喜び楽しみは自分の喜び楽しみと考え、いつもその大本（おおもと）である神の思し召しに従って政治を行う役人が、本当のよい役人である。

4、百姓は、その労力を通して国に尽すことが大事である。生産をあげ、納税の義務や労力の賦課（ふか）等を完全に果（はた）すことが必要である。

5、たとえ代官の命令であっても、それが百姓衆を苦しめる時は、その命令が無理であることを説明して、代官を諫（いさ）める努力をするのがよい役人である。道理にかなったことであれば決して不敬の罪ではなく、役職をいただいている者の大事な節義であるから、このあたりのわきまえが大事であることはいうまでもない。

(二)　横目役大体

1、横目役の第一の仕事は、悪い事をする罪人を出さないことであり、犯人の探し方、捕え方が上手であるとか、尋問の仕方が上手であるなどと言うことは、枝葉のことに過ぎない。

2、鰥寡（かんか）、孤独、老人、子どもなど恵まれない人たちをあわれみ、難儀苦しみにあっている者を助け、人々が互いに助け合うように仕向けることが大事である。

3、罪の軽い者を重く罰したり、罪の重い者を軽く罰したりしないよう、公平に法を遵守(じゅんしゅ)させ、納得させることが大事な役目である。

政照は、西郷帰藩後間もなく与人役に任(にん)じられます。この与人役大体や横目役大体が手本になったことは言うまでもありません。政照は多くの時間を農村見廻りに当て、農民を指導し、励まし、私利私欲を持たず、村民と苦楽を共にします。村民からは、「土持（ツナチ）の主(しゅ)」（土持（ツナチ）を屋号とした。主は政照のこと）と呼ばれ尊敬されていきます。民謡の中でも親しみを持って歌われました。

おひとつ(ティチ)召し上がれ(オイシリ)　土持(ツナチ)の主(シュ)
もう一杯(ナーティーチ)召し上がれ(オイシリ)　土持の主
サイサイ酒持って来い(サイムチク)　飲んで遊ぼう(ヌディアシバ)

与人役が戸長という役職に変わりましたが、政照は三十余年にわたって指導的地位にあり、島の発展に尽しました。敬天愛人思想の第一の実践者と賛えられるべきでしょう。

南洲翁遺訓四

萬民の上に位する者、己れを慎み、品行を正しくし、驕奢(きょうしゃ)を戒め、節倹(せっけん)に勉め、職事に勤労して、人民の標準となり、下民(かみん)其の勤労を気の毒に思う様ならでは、政令は行われ難し。然るに草創(そうそう)の始に立ちながら、家屋を飾り、衣服を文(かざ)り、美妾(びしょう)を抱へ、蓄財を謀(はか)りなば、維新の功業は遂げられ間敷也。今と成りては、戊辰の義戦も偏へに私を営みたる姿に成り行き、天下に対し戦死者に対し面目なきぞとて、頻(しき)りに涙を催されける。

（解釈）人民の上に立つ者は、いつも自分の心をつつしみ、行いを正しくし、おごりや贅沢を戒め、無駄をせず仕事に励んで人々の手本となり、みんながその仕事ぶりや生活を気の毒に思うぐらいにならなければ、政治の命令は行われにくいものである。しかしながら、維新の始めというのに、家を飾ったり衣服をぜいたくにしたり、美妾をかこい、財産を蓄えることばかりを考えるならば、維新の本当の成果を全うすることはできない。今となっては戊辰の正義の戦いもひとえに私利私

欲を肥やす結果となり、国に対し、また戦死者に対して面目ないことだと言って
しきりに涙を流された。

七、備荒貯蓄の教え

西郷は、文久三年の初秋、自ら「与人役大体」「横目役大体」を草して、これを政照に与えました。西郷は、統治牧民の任を帯びて島流しにされたわけではない。一人の罪人としてきたのであるが、島民のより善き生活、いささかでも生き甲斐のある一生を送らせたいということにおいては、代官、役人以上に関心を注いだのでありました。沖永良部島は、四方海に囲まれ、毎年秋に襲来する台風により、塩害を受け、百姓一年の収穫を一日にして皆無にしている。尚また、夏の干ばつによる作物被害も甚大である。その上、隆起珊瑚礁の島であり、土地低く水源となる山らしい山もなく、作物の豊凶を雨露に頼るしかない。台風、干ばつ等の天災による大飢饉の記録が島の歴史を物語っている。

ある日、例によって、政照が座敷牢に行くと、西郷は殊の外にこにこして政照を迎えま

した。

西郷「政照さん、沖永良部の島は、台風や干ばつなど、いろいろな天災が多いようじゃが、若し、これ等の天災等のため、大飢饉になって人々が飢え死にするようになったら、あなたは島民の上に立つ役人として、どのようにして人々を助けますか。」

政照「ご存知の通りの離れ小島でございますから、鹿児島の殿様にお願いして、助けていただくより他によい方法はございません。」

西郷「なる程、あなたが言う通り、沖永良部島は離れ小島です。殿様は、お願いを聞き入れて救援物資を送ってくださるでしょう。でも、台風や季節風が吹いて幾日も船が出ないこともあります。お願いのため鹿児島に行くだけでも何十日もの日数がかかります。生きるか死ぬかの大事な時に、こんなに多くの日数を費やしていては、島民は全部飢え死にしてしまいます。そんな時、島民の生命、財産を預かる役人として、あなたは、どうしますか。」

政照は、返事に困り、ただうなだれるばかりでありました。

それを見て、西郷は、

西郷「そのような非常の時に、一番大事なことは、全島民が心を一つにして、一致協力の体制で、その苦難に当たることですよ。世の中に一致協力ほど強いものはありません。『他人の力に頼る、他人の力にすがる』ということは、失敗のもとです。中国では昔、宋の時代に各々の地域の住民が心を一つにして社倉というものをつくり、そのお陰で数年にわたる大飢饉を切り抜けることができました。沖永良部島でも全島民が心を一つにして飢饉に備える必要があると思われるので、その社倉のつくり方を書いてあげましょう」と言って、社倉趣意書を書いて、政照に与えました。

(一) 社倉（しゃそう）趣意書（抄）

不作、飢饉に対する備えというものは、豊作の年に倹約して穀物を集めて貯蔵しておくことである。貯蔵する穀物の集め方については不公平にならぬよう各農家毎に粟、麦、米の余り高を調べてから、家族数を勘案して割り振りすれば、農民衆の人気もよろしく、自然に社倉の趣旨に基く仁恕（じんじょ）の大事が成しとげられるものである。例えば、集めた米が、皆で五石になった場合、年二割の利子で貸し付けたら一年後には一石の利子が生まれる。更に年を重ねていくと、相当の石高になるので、その場合は、最初に集めた五石は拠出した農民に返して、その後は利子米だけで運用していく。

このようにしていけば、人の不時の災難を救ったり、廃疾（はいしつ）の者をあわれんだりして不幸な人たちを救助する道も開けるのではないか。飢饉に見舞われた場合、困窮（こんきゅう）した人たちにとっては天の賜と有難く思われ、長い間の苦労が報いられることであろう。何と言っても飢饉年になってからあわてないように、前もって備えておくことが大事である。もともと百姓は労力をもって奉仕し、役人は頭と精神を労して奉仕するものである。百姓も役人もその全力を尽して奉仕することが大切である。

㈡　沖永良部社倉設立

政照は、その趣意書に深く感動し、元治元年与人に任じられると、すぐさま同僚や有志に諮（はか）り、その設立を企てたが、次期尚早（しょうそう）として実現せず、六年後の明治三年秋に沖永良部社倉の創設をみました。

事業は、年々順調に進み、ただちに凶年に役立ったばかりでなく、貧困者の救済、公立病院設置、教育費の補助など共済の機関として、顕著な活動をしました。その計画、内容及び経緯は次の通りであります。

○計画と内容

	割当拠出	拠出米、利米の合計	摘要
明治3年	米百石	百石	
明治4年		百二十石	計画通りにならなかったが翌年からの援助でほぼ達成
明治5年		百四十四石	
明治6年		百七十二石八斗	砂糖二十九万二千斤を繰り入れ
明治7年		二百七石三斗六升	千三百三十三円を繰り入れ
明治8年		二百四十八石八斗三升二合	当初の百石を拠出者へ返済
明治9年	純資産百四十八石八斗余で運用開始		

＊凶年には、利息を一割五分にさげるか、無利息にした。

○経緯

明治六年　廃藩置県により保護会社への負債額五十八万四千斤の半額二十九万二千斤を免除、半額を社倉へ繰り入れた。

明治七年　県庁より五万貫（千三百三十三円）を貸与。社倉へ繰り入れた。

明治八年　社倉資金で鹿児島へ留学生派遣

医学生（三年間）沖縜賢、鎌田宗圓、操坦勁

伝習生（一年間）坂本元明、東一徳、栄寿祥

明治九年　社倉支所創設（高倉）玉城、上平川、芦清良、瀬利覚、田舎平、下城

明治十四年　九月畦布村に疑似コレラ発生
　　　　　　窮民救済防疫救助
明治十六年　公立病院建設
　　　　　　医院長　沖利有
　　　　　　副医院長　撰玄碩
　　　　　　医師　皆吉庸熙、福山清道、栄寿祥
明治十八年　十二月火災により病院焼失
明治十九年　十一月未曾有の暴風雨襲来
　　　　　　罹災者四百十六人に社倉資金及び官米を支出し救助した。
明治二十七年　和泊港改修　社倉千五百円、県補助千八百円援助
明治三十三年　汽船就航、電信開通により、社倉備蓄の必要がなくなり解散となった。
明治三十四年　解散時の資金により左記の記念碑建立
　　　　　　○西郷隆盛謫居之地碑
　　　　　　○西郷神社建立（資金の一部）
明治三十九年　○土持政照彰徳碑

八、報恩丸建造

「生麦事件」と「薩英戦争」とは

島津久光公が、徳川幕府に幕政改革の勅命を伝達に行く勅使大原重徳を護衛して、江戸に行きました。そして、慶喜を後見職に、松平慶永を政事総裁職にすることを幕府に決定させ、その使命を果して京都へ帰る途中、文久二年八月二十一日の午後、横浜市鶴見区生麦にさしかかったとき、乗馬のイギリス商人リチャードソンら四人と出会った。ところが、その乗馬の一頭が大名行列の中にはいりこんで混乱が起こった。行列の供頭をつとめていた奈良原喜左衛門は、無礼だと、抜刀してリチャードソンを斬り殺し、ほかの男性二人を負傷させたのである。これが、生麦事件の概略である。

イギリスは、生麦事件に怒った。幕府に対し謝罪と賠償金十万ポンドを、薩摩藩に対しては、犯人引渡しと、遺族への慰謝料二万五千ポンドを要求した。幕府は、要求に応じたものの、薩摩藩は、いずれも拒否した。その後、交渉も行われたが、解決に至らず、イギリス代理公使ジョン・ニールは、武力に頼るしかないと判断、イギリス艦隊を翌年の文久三年六月二十七日、ユーリアス号ほか六隻の軍艦を鹿児島錦江湾に向かわせた。二十八、二十九日の両日、交渉は続けられたが、イギリス、薩摩双方一歩も譲らず、七月二日朝、開戦となった。これが薩英戦争である。（鹿児島県史及び東郷實晴著『西郷隆盛―その生涯』による。）

文久三年秋の終わりごろ、西郷は社倉趣意書を書き終え、政照に与え、その後、静かな牢生活を送っていました。が、突然、鹿児島で薩英戦争が起こったという知らせを受けました。伝えられてきた薩英戦争の内容は、何倍もの噂となったものでした。英国軍は、数十隻の軍艦を以って鹿児島湾に侵入し、城下は殆ど焼き払われ、薩摩の船はことごとく撃沈され、戦死者も多数に及んだとか、幕府がイギリスを後押ししているとか、その他一つとして薩摩の有利を伝えたものはありませんでした。

西郷は居ても立っても居られなかった。殊に幕府がイギリスと結んで、薩摩を攻めたということには心を痛めた。

西郷の心は、千々に乱れて出るのはため息ばかりでありました。

政照はいつものとおり、牢に西郷を訪ねました。

政照「先生、何か心配ごとがあるんじゃないですか、私にも聞かせてください。」
西郷「政照さん、よいところへ来てくれました。実は、鹿児島で戦争が起こったというのですよ。イギリス軍が砲撃をしかけてきて、鹿児島の町は焼野原となり、死傷者も多く出ているようです。気が気でなりません。たとえ私は罪を重ねるようなことがあっても、一刻も早く鹿児島へ上り、役に立てないものかと考えていたところです。」
政照「鹿児島では戦争が起こっているのですか、私も父が鹿児島におります。心配ですので、いっしょに連れて行ってください。」

西郷は脱出するための船が欲しいと考えていたが、よい手立てがない。思い切って政照に相談をしました。

政照は、切羽詰(せっぱつま)った西郷の話を聞き、「その船は、私が造りましょう」と約束しました。

政照は、そのことを、母お鶴に打ち明けました。お鶴は、「お前は自分の子ながら、実に見上げたものだ。船を造るお金のことは、この母も協力します。女の拵(こしら)えた船は運が強いそうですから。」政照母子は嬉し泣きに泣きました。

お鶴は、これまで実の親子同然に生活し奉公してきた二人の雇い人を呼んで、鹿児島の戦争のことや、西郷の祖国の危急を救うための船建造の費用のことを話し、金をつくるための奉公替えを、涙を流しながらお願いしました。二人は温かいご当家を離れることは死ぬよりつらいことだけど、西郷先生や皆さんのためなら奉公替えをさせてください。受けたご高恩は一生肝に銘じ、子々孫々まで伝えていきます、と言い二人に各々屋子母村、皆川村へ奉公替えをしてもらい、お金の目処はつきました。

西郷は嬉しかった。わが西郷家にも雇い人は数人いるが、なかなかできることではないであろうと思いをめぐらせつつ、土持家の義挙、誠忠に対して感謝の詩を作って政照に与えました。

贈土持政照

精神滅せず昔人の清きに、
専ら君恩を顧みて壮気横たわる。
眼を開き船を営りて真意顕われ、
涙を揮い僕をひきいで俗縁軽し。
北堂の貞訓能く応に奉ずべく、

先祖の忠勤当に力行すべし。
畢世勉めよや国事に酬い、
無私純忠　群英に挺でんことを。

（解釈）あなたの真心は、昔の人の気高い精神に少しも劣らない。誠心誠意、主恩に報いようと気概に燃えている。広く世界の情勢に目を向け、船の造営に打ち込む姿に真情がよく見られるし、涙を振り払って下僕を売り資金調達をしたことは、並みの縁の断ち切り方ではない。ご母堂の教えをよく守って、ご先祖さまの忠勤ぶりに負けない立派なはたらきに精出してほしい。生涯つとめ励んでもらいたいものだ。国事に尽力し、公平無私、純真で遠大な志の優れた人たちより抜きんでることを祈る。

西郷は、船を造るための大木のある官有林の払い下げを願書にしたため、政照名で代官に提出しました。それによると、①島に外国が侵攻してきた時、援兵を鹿児島に願い出るための船、②鹿児島に変乱が起こった時、島を脱出して行けるようにするための船、の二点が主な目的となっています。「船材払下げ願書」は、直ちに許可され、官有林伐採、船建造に着手することになりました。船は十一月初旬完成し、報恩丸と命名されました。

そんな中、たまたま琉球通いの商船が寄港し、薩英戦争の結末を知らせました。西郷は、更に詳細について、沖縄の米良助右衛門等に書簡を送り、問い合わせています。それにより明らかになったことは、「七月二日朝、藩が重富沖にかくしていた汽船天佑丸ほか二隻を捕えられ焼かれてしまった。船長五代友厚と寺島宗則は部下を逃がした後、進んで捕りょとなり、イギリス艦隊と共に横浜に連れて行かれた。そこで藩も開戦命令を出し、各砲台は一斉に火をふいた。桜島の横山砲台近くに碇泊していた英艦一隻は、不意をつかれて錨をあげるひまもなく、錨の鎖を切って逃げるしまつであった。旗艦ユリアス号の艦橋に、わが方の砲弾が炸裂して艦長と副艦長ほか数人が即死した。戦闘は台風が吹き荒れる二日と翌三日と続いたが、四日に艦隊は退去していった。

この戦争でわが方の受けた損害は、戦死十人、負傷十一人、城下の民家五百戸焼失し、幾つかの砲台と集成館が破壊され、汽船三隻と和船数隻を失った」とのことでした。（その後は、薩摩は賠償金などを支払い、友好関係を築き、留学生十九人をイギリスへ送っている。記念碑「若き薩摩の群像」鹿児島市。）この確かな情報が座敷牢内の西郷に届いたのは、二か月余り過ぎた十月

“若き薩摩の群像”碑

の初めごろでした。苦心惨たんして造った報恩丸も初期の目的に使う必要はなくなったが、与人操坦栽（たんさい）が薩英戦争慰問使（いもんし）として鹿児島に上るため、これを使用することになりました。

慰問使になった坦栽は、戦争の見舞い旁（かたがた）、藩庁へ、この沖永良部島にも大砲を備えてくださるようお願いしたいと思うので、その嘆願書の原稿を書いてくださいと西郷にお願いしました。西郷は、早速筆をとって、その草稿を書き坦栽に渡しました。その草稿の内容は、相手の立場を極（わきま）えながら、心を尽し丁寧な表現の文章でありました。ここでは、その要旨のみにとどめておくことにします。

①若し外敵が襲来した場合、充分な防御（ぼうぎょ）ができない時は、只沖永良部島の汚名だけでは

“報恩丸” 模型

済まないと心配でなりません。

②離島である沖永良部島にまで軍備をお願いすることは誠に恐縮ですが、差し当たり十文筒拾丁ぐらいお差し渡しください。

③都合がつき兼ねる場合は、せめて一丁でも欲しい。代金は、春の砂糖を以ってお納めします。

文久三年　亥　十一月二十八日

操坦栽は、間もなくして上国をいたしましたが、その際西郷は次の和歌二首を餞（はなむけ）として送りました。

君がため　深き海原行く船を
あらくな　吹きそ　しなとへの神

諸人の誠のつもる船なれば
行くも帰るも　神や守らん

九、義兄弟の契り

西郷がこの島に流されてから早一年余り、獄窓の明け暮れに、片時も離れないものは、政照のこまやかでしみじみと心に染みわたる情誼であります。もし、政照がいなかったら、とっくに自分は死んで、沖永良部島の土になっていただろうと思い、彼は政照を見るたびに「有難さ」「なつかしさ」に胸のつまる思いでいっぱいでありました。この頃になって、政照と兄弟の縁を結びたいという気持ちが、しきりに西郷の胸中を往来していました。会えば会うほど、語れば語るほど、二人の意気は相投合していきました。西郷は、ためらいもなく政照に手紙を書きました。

「今夜、いろいろお願いしたいことがあるので、ぜひ、母上といっしょに酒と肴を用意して座敷牢に来ていただきたい。」　政照は、西郷が自ら酒肴を要求したのは初めてのことで、大変嬉しかった。母お鶴も大変喜んで、腕によりをかけて酒肴を準備し、座敷牢を訪ねました。

西郷「お母さん、ご面倒をかけてすみませんでした。政照さんは、私の大事な命の恩人です。半分死にかかっていた私を助けてくださった命の恩人でございます。そのお陰で、私は九死に一生を得ることができました。これ全く、政照さんのお陰でございます。」

お鶴「折角お側近くにいながら政照は行き届かないことばかりで申し訳次第もございません。」

芯を二つ点(とも)した行灯(あんどん)は、格子をはさんで座った三人の顔を明々と照らしています。喜びのうちに献酬(けんしゅう)が始まりました。やがて西郷は居住居(いずまい)を正してお鶴に話し始めました。

西郷「お母さん、実は今夜は折入ってあなた方親子にお願いしたいことがあって、お出でをお願いしたわけです。政照さんは、私にとって命の恩人であります。何から何まで痒(かゆ)い所に手が届くように親切にしてもらい、他人とは思えません。どうかお母さん、今日から二人を兄弟にしてください。お願いします。」

お鶴「いたらぬ政照を、それほどまでに……。勿体ないことです。有難いことです。旦那様、どうかお願いします。政照を先生の弟分にしてください。」

政照「先生、本当に勿体ないことで、有難うございます。」
西郷「お許しくださいまして有難うございます。それでは、お母さん、私に盃を一つください。」
お鶴はあまりの嬉しさに、ふるえる手で囲いの中の西郷に盃を差し上げました。西郷は、その盃をお鶴に返しながら言いました。「今日からどうか、この私もあなたの本当の子供だと思ってください。」
西郷「政照さん、つまらない男ではあるが、私が年上だから兄になりますよ」と言いながら西郷は別の盃を政照に差し上げました。
政照「先生！　いや兄さん、こんな嬉しいことはありません。」
西郷「それでは、お母さん、親兄弟の盃はすみました。これで、政照と二人は義兄弟になりました。記念に大島で習い覚えた歌を一つ歌いましょう。」
♪我身（わみ）やくぬ島に　親はろじ居（う）らむ
我ぬ愛（かな）しゃしゅしどぅ　我親はろじ
（私はこの島に親や親戚はいない　私を可愛がってくれる人が私の親、親戚です。）
お鶴「私も一つ今夜の歓びを歌いましょう。」

♪旅ぬ人どぅやしが　がに愛しゃあろや
肝からがやゆら　縁からがやゆら
（よその人であるのにどうしてこんなに親しいのであろうか　心がぴったり合ったからであろうか。それとも昔からの縁なのであろうか。）

政照「私も歌いましょう。」

♪植いてあぬ松ぬ老木なるまでぃむ
さとぅ我ぬ縁ぬ　続ち給り
（植えてある松の苗木が老木になるまでも二人の縁が長続きしますように。）

三人の歓喜は、その絶頂に達しました。西郷は立ち上がって硯と紙を取り出し、さらさらと書き流して「完全な漢詩にはなっていませんが、私の心を表したものです。今夜の記念に差し上げましょう」と言って、政照に手渡しました。

時に西郷三十七歳、政照二十八歳でありました。

平素眼前　皆平かならず、

情の相適する時情と異なり。
安を偸(ぬす)み義に悖(もと)るは九寇(きゅうこう)の如く、
欲を禁じ忠を効(いた)すには死生(しせい)を共にす。
余(われ)君に許し君も也(また)我に許す、
弟(てい)は兄(けい)と称し弟を却(かえ)って兄と称す。
従来の交誼(こうぎ)は何事なるかを知らん、
国に報いんとて身を輸(いた)して至誠を尽すなり。

（解釈）　ふだん目にふれるものごとには、気に入らないことが多いのだが、あなたとの心の通い合いは、並の情愛とはまるで違っていた。言葉を貪(むさぼ)り道義に外れた行いをする者は仇敵のように忌(い)み嫌(きら)い、私欲を抑え真心を尽す人とは生涯生死を共にしたいもの。私はあなたに真底(しんそこ)心を許し、あなたもまた真底心を許してきた、年下の私があなたを兄と呼べば年上のあなたも私を兄と呼んだ。これまでの厚い交友は一体何事だったのかと言えば、国に報い人のため身を挺(てい)して至誠を尽すことだったのだ。

文久三年五月天下の情勢は、公武合体派と尊攘派の対立が、激化の様相を呈しておりました。長州藩においては、尊攘派の勢力が強く下関海峡を通過するアメリカの商船や、フランス、オランダの軍艦を砲撃し攘夷を実力行使によって示しております。これに対し、アメリカやフランスは幕府に抗議するとともに、下関に砲撃を加え多大な損害を与える報復に出てきます。孝明天皇は、尊攘より公武合体を熱望され、会津藩の松平容保、越前藩の松平慶永、そして、薩摩藩の島津久光、大久保利通らとその対策を練っていました。その結果、尊攘派の三条実美ら七人の公卿と御所の守護に当たっていた長州藩は退けられ長州へ落ちのびていきました。世に言う「八・一八政変」であります。これにより、薩摩と会津を中心とした公武合体運動が、しばらく続くことになりました。

京都を追われた長州は薩摩、会津を薩賊会奸と呼び薩摩と長州は険悪になっていきます。その後、薩摩でも公武合体派と尊攘派の対立が激化し、新しい指導者の出現が痛切に感じはじめられました。

＊　公武合体　朝廷（天皇）と幕府がいっしょになって政を行う。

＊　尊攘（尊王攘夷）　外国を排除し天皇の権能を強くし、朝廷のもとに政を行う。

南洲翁遺訓二十

何程制度方法を論ずる共、其の人に非ざれば行われ難し。人有て後方法の行わるるものなれば、人は第一の宝にして、己れ其の人に成るの心懸け肝要なり。

（解釈）どんな制度や方法を論じたとしても、説く人が立派でなければことはうまく行われない。立派な人があってはじめて方法は行われるものだから、人こそ第一の宝であって、自分がそういう立派な人物になるよう心懸けることが何より大事なことである。

十、「西郷の赦免」運動起こる

薩英戦争で襲撃を受けた薩摩は、精忠組を中心に幕府に対し反感を持ち始めました。即ち、薩英戦争の原因である生麦事件について、幕府はイギリス側の抗議におののき、怖れて、その責任を薩摩に押し付けてしまったのです。

薩摩は、このことは藩のみならず日本国そのものの存亡に関わる重大問題とし、この難局を乗り切る人物は、沖永良部島謫居（たっきょ）中の西郷以外にはないとの結論に達しました。精忠組そして寺田屋事件に連座した同志たちも賛同して、西郷赦免を嘆願する運動を起こしました。（寺田屋事件とは、京都寺田屋で藩内尊攘派の精忠組の同志を上意討ちにした事件。）

しかし、久光公の西郷に対する憎悪（ぞうお）の念は、ちっとやそっとでは消えない強いものがあります。

元治元（一八六四）年正月、京都詰めの薩摩藩士、福山清蔵、井上弥八郎、高崎正風（せいふう）、高崎猪太郎、永山弥一郎、篠原国幹（くにもと）、黒田清綱等十三名の志士たちが集って、西郷赦免の議を久光公に具申（ぐしん）し、若し容（い）れられない場合は、君前において直ちに割腹（かっぷく）することを申し合わせました。みんなの代表を高崎正風に決めました。

高崎正風は、久光にお目通りをして、天下の情勢を説き、どうしても西郷を赦免して呼び戻すよう嘆願しました。

久光は、銀の煙管（きせる）で煙草を吸いながら聞いていましたが、返事をしません。煙管をくわえたまま振り向きもしません。いかにも苦い顔をしています。高崎はひるんだが、勇気を出して更に切言しました。久光はなお黙っていましたが、高崎はあくまでも退去しないで平伏を続けていると、はじめて口の煙管をとって、言いました。

「君たちの言う処によれば、誰もが西郷は賢者だと言っているが、それでは久光一人が愚かで、君たちの願いを聞かないでいることは、みんなのためにならないことになる。太守公（藩主忠義公）の裁決を仰がれよ」と折れてくれました。この時、久光がくわえていた煙管の吸口に深い歯の跡がついたという。腹立たしさの余り銀煙管をかんで西郷の召還を悔しがったと言うのである。藩士一同は天に飛び上がらんばかりに喜び、西郷呼び戻しの使者に吉井友実、西郷従道、福山清蔵の三人が決まりました。時に文久四（一八六四）年一月下旬のことでありました。

十一、迎えの汽船「胡蝶丸」沖永良部島へ

西郷赦免運動は、文久三年七月に起こった薩英戦争後急速に高まってきました。西郷も叔父椎原権兵衛らの便りで、近いうちに赦免され帰藩できるかも知れないという知らせを受けていました。心中、喜んで胸おどらせていたのであったが、決して冷静さを失うこと

はありませんでした。沖永良部島へ遠島処分を受けたとき、もはや命はないものと死を覚悟し、すべてを天命と受けとめ、どんな苦難苦行にも耐え抜いてきたのであります。天は西郷をこの島で生かし続け、時の到来を待たせたのであります。

西郷赦免正使（せいし）・吉井友実ら三人が乗った汽船胡蝶丸が島に着いたのは元治元（一八六四）年二月二十一日でした。そのころ、鹿児島には天然痘（てんねんとう）が流行しており、各島では島内に流行させないため、鹿児島からの船が入港した時は役人が検疫（けんえき）を行い、疑いのある者は上陸させないよう予防措置をとっていました。

政照はこの日、飛脚船が伊延に着いたので、船員の検疫のため伊延港へ馬を走らせていました。途中、書状を携えて走ってくる船子に出会いました。尋ねてみると、何とその書状は、西郷の赦免状でありました。西郷様を迎える船のことなども話してくれました。政照は矢立てを取り出して「先生、今日あたりお迎えの船が来るらしい、私も検疫をすませたら、牢に急行します」と認（したた）めて、これは西郷殿へとどけてください、と船子に矢立てを依頼して伊延に馬を走らせました。

検疫の最中、黒煙をあげながら徳之島から本島へ向かってくる船影が見えます。まさしく汽船胡蝶丸でした。政照は急いで検疫をすませ一目散に和泊へ馳（は）せ帰り、検疫の報告をする間ももどかしく、座敷牢を訪ねました。西郷は既に礼服に着替えて牢屋に座っておられます。「先生、お迎えの船がやがて港に着きますよ、早く牢を出てください」と急がせます。

西郷は「さっきは書面をありがとうございました。あれからすぐ山田代官が来られて赦免状を読んで聞かせてくださいました」と言われ、動こうとしない西郷の手を無理やりとって連れ出し、近くの岩の高見に上って海の向こうを見遣(みや)っています。船は国頭(くにがみ)岬近くを廻って和泊港へ向かっているようです。今度は西郷が慌(あわ)て出しました。二人はすぐさま牢に引き返し、窪一と共に荷造りに取りかかります。

政照「先生、何をそんなに探しておられるのですか。」

西郷「着古しではありますが、先君斉彬公から戴いた縞縮緬(しまちりめん)の袷(あわせ)を、あなたに形見にあげようと思って、さっきから探しているのですが、一向に見つかりません。何処に置いたのでしょうか。」

政照「先生、先生の腋下(わきした)に挟(はさ)んでいらっしゃる物は何ですか。」

西郷「あっはっはあ、これ、これ、腋下に挟んでいるから、いくら探しても見つからんはずじゃ。」

いくら沈着冷静な西郷でも、この時ばかりは落ちつかない心の動揺が政照にも見て取れました。西郷は、この袷を丁寧に政照に差し上げました。

胡蝶丸は丸に十の字の藩旗と日の丸をはためかせ、しぶきを上げながら、一直線に海の向こうから長浜（ながはま）目がけて走ってきます。浜に集まった大ぜいの人々はわいわいがやがや、船の入ってくる方向を見ています。西郷と政照の二人は感極まって声が出ません。二人の眼には涙がいっぱいにたまっていました。

天は、南海の孤島で心を洗われた西郷に時の到来を告げ、大任の命（めい）を下したのでした。

胡蝶丸が錨をおろしたのは、午後一時を少し過ぎたころでした。本船からのボートは従道ら三人を乗せ、波間を浮き沈みしながら長浜に近づいてきます。従道はボートが浜に着き板はしごを懸けるのも待たずに砂浜にとび下り、出迎えの群衆の中を一目散に兄・吉之助の所へ走り寄ります。

従道「兄さん。」

西郷「おお、来たか。」

西郷は大きな両手で弟の手をひしと握りしめ、後は声が出ません。二人ともうつ向いたまま、はらはらと大粒の涙を流します。そばにいる出迎えの人たちも誰一人として仰ぎ見

る者もなく、すすり泣きの声が聞かれます。西郷はしばらくして涙を払い、吉井の方を向いて、

西郷「おお、ヨゴレ、ワイ（お前）も来たか。」

吉井「ばかなことを言いヤンナ、オイ（俺）はお前を迎えに来た正使ジャッド、ヨゴレチューワ、何チューコッカ。」

西郷は政照の方をふり向いて、

西郷「コイワナ、稚児ンコロカラ、ヨゴレッオッシテナ、シラミ五郎チューテ、腕白モンゴワシター。」

一同どっと大笑いしてなごやかな雰囲気に変わりました。一通りの挨拶を交わし終えると、西郷は、吉井に話されます。

西郷「喜界島に流されている村田新八も一緒に帰るんだろうな。」

吉井「今度はあなただけです。」

西郷「それはいかん、俺だけ帰るわけにはいかん。村田は俺よりうんと罪は軽いんだ。俺より先に許されるべきだ。よし、村田を連れて帰ろう。船を喜界に廻せ、責任は俺が持つ」と断言しました。自分の好事よりも友を思いやる心が強かったのである。

吉井らも西郷の心中はよく察知しており、共に帰ることに同意したのでありました。迎えの三人は一週間程島に滞在して、島のことや、人々の暮らし、民情等視察して帰るつもりでしたが、石炭が残り少なくなったので、翌日帰ることにしました。西郷は島の人たちに別れの挨拶をして廻り、お世話になった人々に形見の品を分け与えています。政照母子には牢で使った斉彬公拝領の桐の火鉢や着物を贈っています。鹿児島から持参してきた物は殆んど、お礼や形見として島の人々に分けてやりました。その夜は、与人役所で送別の宴が開かれました。迎えの三人も招かれ、山田代官、詰役、島役人はじめ主だった人々が集まっています。召還を喜ぶ者、別れを惜しむ者、悲喜こもごもの状況で宴はにぎわいました。西郷は、懐から紙を取り出し、別れの漢詩を書いて政照に手渡しました。

政照子に留別（りゅうべつ）す

別離夢の如く又雲の如し、
去らんと欲して還り来て涙泫沄（げんうん）。
獄裡の仁恩　謝するに語無く、
遠く波浪を凌（しの）いで痩（や）せて君を思わん。

（解釈）お別れは夢のようでまた雲のようで、はかなくも落ちつかない。立ち去ろうと思ってはまた後戻りして涙がとめどなく流れる。牢屋暮らしで受けた数々のご恩には感謝のことばもありません。鹿児島に帰っても遠く海をへだててやせる思いで君のことを偲（しの）びます。

別れの宴も次第に惜別の情で包まれていきます。西郷や従道、福山らは吉井にせき立てられて、会場を辞することになりました。長浜ではいくつもの松明（たいまつ）があかあかと焚かれて多くの人々が一行を見送ろうと待ち受けています。板はしごを伝って西郷一行が艀（はしけ）に乗り移ると、「先生、さようなら」「お元気で」………大きな歓声が響きわたります。その中にひときわ「先生……先生、お元気で」と絶叫する者がいました。「おお、島富（しまとみ）か……来てくれたか、おおきに……おおきに、世話になってありがとう……もうここにはもう何もなかで（ないので）……これを形見に……お礼のしるしじゃ取っといてくれ」と叫びながら着ている肌衣（はだぎ）を脱いで帯でしばって砂浜に投げてやりました。

長田島富は、この日、畑仕事を途中で切り上げ帰宅していたところ役所からの連絡を受け、急いで国頭村から駆けつけたのでした。島富は、西郷の在島中、窪一とともに、飯炊きの仕事など、世話をしていました。

西郷や迎えに来た三人を乗せた艀は、みんなに見送られ、本船胡蝶丸に向かいます。胡蝶丸が錨を上げ龍郷向けて出港したのは、翌二十二日午前一時ごろでした。

十二、帰還後に

(一) 奄美の黒糖地獄を救う

明治維新の偉業は、西郷らの大活躍で成し遂げられ、自由な近代国家建設へと時代は移行していきますが、奄美の黒糖財政は以前のまま取り残されていました。藩政時代にかかえた農民の借財は、そのまま県へ返済せねばならなかったのです。旧薩摩藩では保護会社をつくって黒糖を一片残さず安値で買い上げ、高値で全国に売りさばき、農民へは高値で日用品等を下げ渡し、莫大な利益を得ていたのでした。農民は不作の年は、来年の砂糖を抵当にして、高い利息で保護会社から金を借り、積もり積もった返済に四苦八苦していたのです。

明治五年、砂糖は自由売買になりましたが、新法下において地租税が賦課され、二重の支拂いに窮することになってしまいました。

沖永良部島の場合、旧保護会社への負債額は百四十六万斤、地租税が三十一万斤となっています。全島の一年間の製糖額が百四十万斤なので、ほぼ負債額に等しい。このまま負債額をかかえていては、島の財政は破綻してしまうと考えた与人政照は、県庁に負債額の減額と年賦償還陳情のため鹿児島へ上りました。上京中だった大山綱良県令から「すぐ上京せよ」との電報をもらい、すぐさま東京へ向かいました。東京では大山県令から、西郷(筆頭参議)を訪ねるよう指示され、西郷宅に伺いました。西郷は政照の来訪を涙を流して喜ばれました。政照が戊辰戦について祝意を述べると、西郷は「維新の大業はすべて天下の尊皇忠士の心血の賜であって、自分の力はいささかも加わっていない。しかしながら、もし、この偉業に自分の力も幾分加わっているとしたら、それは決して自分の力ではなく、あなたの功績である」と心底から命の恩人政照に功績をゆずっています。政照は西郷の謙虚さに涙を流して聞いていました。

政照が奄美の黒糖納税等について話をしますと、西郷は、租税権頭(現財務大臣)松方正義宛への手紙をしたため政照に託しました。

その後、手紙を携え、大山県令の了解を得て、松方を訪ね手紙を手渡しました。その結果、租税は軽減され、旧保護会社への負債は六分棄却、四分は三年年賦上納と大幅な譲歩を引き出すことに成功しました。このことは、沖永良部島のみならず奄美の各島々にも適応されることになりました。

大山県令は、その後奄美の各島を巡視され、予想以上の窮乏の生活状況を目にして、三年年賦についても「納付に及ばず、これは別個に積み立てて不作に備えよ」と指令を出しました。すべて西郷の英断の賜であります。これまでの奄美の虐げられてきた農民の苦しみや生活権さえ脅かされてきたことへの償いとして、幾分なりとも救ってやりたいと尽力してくれた西郷の真心に政照は感謝しながら帰郷の途につきました。

(二) 皆吉庸熙・鎌田宗圓　西南の役に従軍

皆川村の皆吉庸熙（皆吉龍馬の祖父）は撰玄碩医師のもとで漢方の医術を学んでいたが、明治七年鹿児島に上り足立盛至医師のもとで西洋医学を勉強していました。

明治八年になると鎌田宗圓、操坦勁、沖揖賢（三名とも沖永良部島での西郷先生の塾生）が医術生として鹿児島へ留学派遣されました。修行年限は三年間です。しかし明治十年になると鹿児島城下は騒然となり、操と沖は修行途中で帰郷せざるを得なくなります。外科、内科の皆吉と鎌田は西南の役で西郷軍に従軍し、負傷兵の治療に当たります。熊本高瀬の激戦で西郷菊次郎は右足に砲弾を受け重傷を負いました。皆吉は足立医師と共に菊次郎の治療に当たりました。

その後皆吉も鎌田も政府軍に捕えられ、懲役三年の判決を受けますが、裁判所は彼らの医術を生かすべく、十年八月三十日に釈放します。西郷は、菊次郎の治療をしてくれた皆吉に鉄砲袖のシャツを謝礼として贈っています。皆吉、鎌田の西南の役参戦は、西郷へのご恩返しとして讃えられるべきでありましょう。

㈢　伝習生の留学派遣

明治維新により政府は明治五年八月学制発布を行いました。沖永良部島では、明治八年になってようやく和泊村に仮学校一校が開設されました。その二年後の明治十年に十六の集落に仮学校が誕生しました。国頭、畦布、花実、玉城、内城、皆川、余多、平川、清良、覚知、徳風、島尻、田皆、下城、後蘭、永誉の十六仮学校です。しかし、生徒数も少なく、教師もやや不足ぎみでした。県は、教師はできるだけ地元登用をすすめました。幸い本島は私塾が多かったため教師の確保はそれほどの困難はなかったものの、将来の教育の充実を図るため、伝習生を鹿児島に留学派遣することにしました。選考されたのは、坂本元明、東一徳、栄寿祥の三名で修業期間は一年、明治八年のことでした。この費用も前述の医学生派遣と共に、社倉資金からの支出でありました。

㈣　田皆(たみな)村に西郷神社建立

沖永良部島で入牢中の西郷の食事や身の回りの世話をした人が、田皆村の田中窪一という人でした。彼は牢内外の掃除、トイレの汲み出し、風呂の準備など懇切丁寧に西郷に尽しました。

西郷が鹿児島へ帰られてのこと、窪一は、商用で鹿児島へ上り、黒砂糖を手土産に上之園町の西郷を訪ねます。西郷は大変喜んで窪一を歓待し、大好きな温泉へ誘います。姶良(あいら)の妙見塩浸(みょうけんしおひたし)温泉で三日間楽しく過ごします。

帰りには土産に衣類、やかん、毛筆の書などを柳行李に積めて持たせます。ところが船に同乗した客たちが、その土産品を欲しがり、気のいい窪一は、惜しげもなく次から次へと分けてあげます。しまいには田皆の家にまで押しかけて来る者もいて、残ったものは、

茶器　急須

やかんと急須の二品だけになりました。（現在和泊西郷南洲記念館に展示してあります。）

明治三十四年、吾館（あかたじ）村（手々知名）に西郷神社が建立されました。西郷の命日九月二十四日には、窪一は、親戚一同揃って一重一瓶（いちじゅういちびん）を持って田皆村から吾館村まで遠い道のりを歩いて来て、吾館村の人たちと共に西郷の供養を続けております。年が経（た）つにつれて通う人たちが少なくなり、神社を田皆にも建てて村中みんなで祭事を地元で行うことになりました。場所は、田皆中学校東隣の高チジに決まり、立派な社殿が建立されました。命日には、盛んに祭事が行われました。ふだんは子どもたちが境内で遊んだり、夕涼みの場所となったり憩いの名所となりました。現在は神社もなくなり、高チジの面影さえなくなってしまいましたが、西郷と田中窪一さんの親交の深さは今でも人々の間に伝えられています。（西口福恒先生のお話から引用させてもらいました。）

(五)　和泊西郷南洲顕彰会の創立

昭和五十二年、西郷南洲没後百年祭を機に西郷南洲翁の遺訓と遺徳を顕彰し、現代社会に高揚する目的で和泊西郷南洲顕彰会を創立した。会員八百四十名、初代会長武田恵喜光氏。各集落に世話人を選出した。この会の事業は次の通り（平成二十九年現在）

ア、研修会の開催　イ、読み物の発行　ウ、展示会　エ、西郷先生ゆかりの地の視察・交流研修　オ、例祭（偲ぶ会）

※交流研修を積極的に推進努力しています。島外より本島に来てもらっているのが現状です。特に山形・荘内南洲会からは、昭和五十二年から毎年、また隔年に「南洲翁の遺徳を訪ねる旅」で来島してもらって交流を深めています。これまでの相互交流先は次の通りです。

山　形　荘内南洲会
東　京　敬天愛人フォーラム21　薩摩士魂の会

千　葉　春風塾
京　都　盛和塾
熊　本　三州会
都　城　庄内会
出　水　敬天昌厳会
鹿児島　西郷南洲顕彰会

西郷家系図

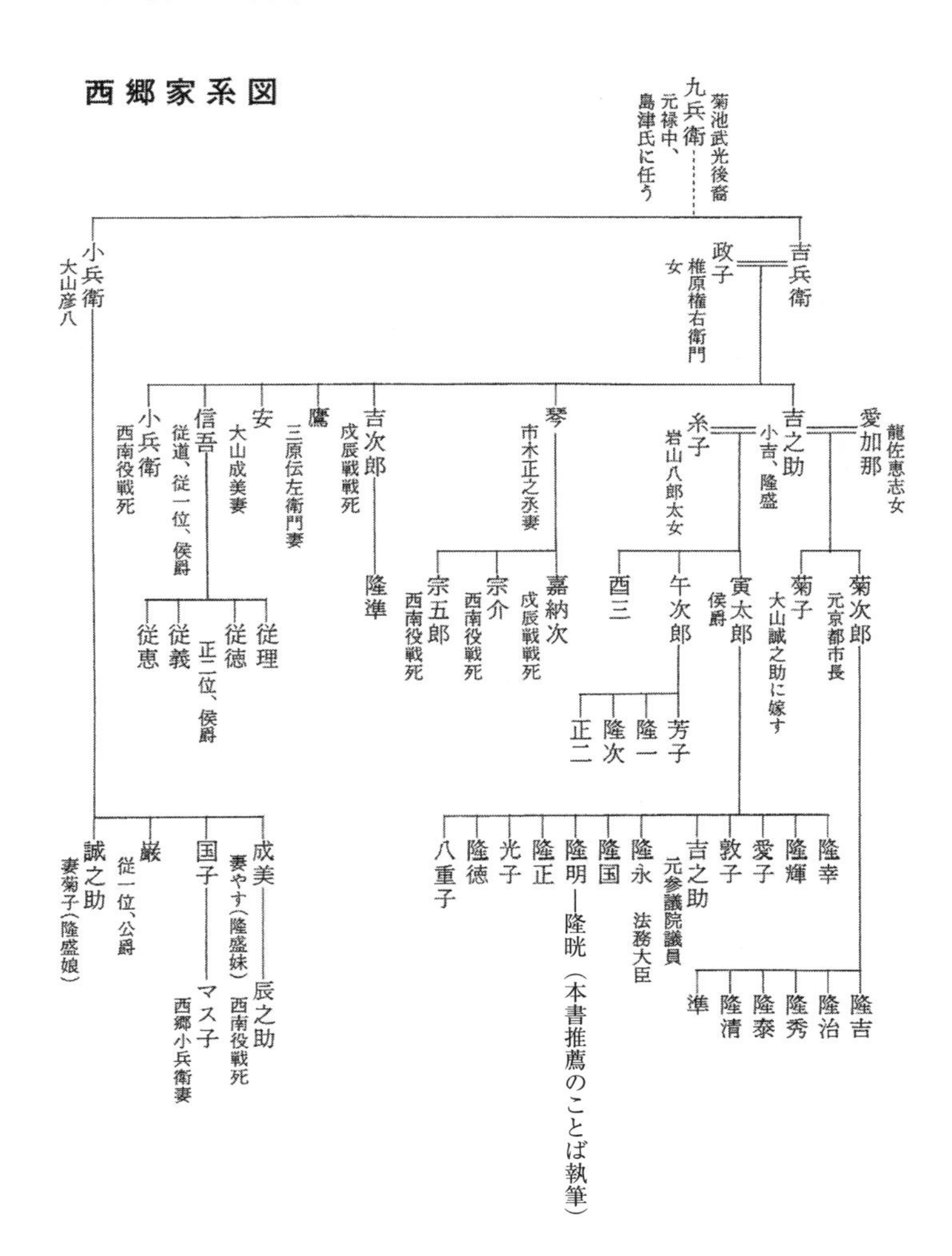
菊池武光後裔
九兵衛
元禄中、島津氏に任う
吉兵衛
政子
椎原権右衛門女
小兵衛
大山彦八
愛加那
龍佐恵志女
吉之助
小吉、隆盛
糸子
岩山八郎太女
琴
市木正之丞妻
吉次郎
戊辰戦戦死
鷹
三原伝左衛門妻
安
大山成美妻
信吾
従道、従一位、侯爵
小兵衛
西南役戦死
菊次郎
元京都市長
菊子
大山誠之助に嫁す
寅太郎
侯爵
午次郎
酉三
嘉納次
戊辰戦戦死
宗介
西南役戦死
宗五郎
西南役戦死
隆準
従理
従徳
正二位、侯爵
従義
従恵
芳子
隆一
隆次
正二
隆幸
隆輝
愛子
敦子
吉之助
元参議院議員
隆永
法務大臣
隆国
隆明
隆晄（本書推薦のことば執筆）
隆正
光子
隆徳
八重子
隆吉
隆治
隆秀
隆泰
隆清
準
成美
妻やす（隆盛妹）
辰之助
西南役戦死
国子
マス子
西郷小兵衛妻
巌
従一位、公爵
誠之助
妻菊子（隆盛娘）

西郷隆盛上陸之地
鹿児島県知事寺園勝志書

昭和三年和泊小学校長玉江末駒氏が、将来子どもたちの教育に役立つという信念のもと、教育関係者を中心に資金を集め、コンクリート製の柱に「西郷隆盛上陸の地」として建立した。昭和二十年大型台風襲来により倒壊してしまった。

現在の石碑は昭和三十八年に建立されたものである。「教育の町」宣言の根拠をなしている、裏面には

西郷隆盛は先に徳之島謫居中の処、更に島替えの命に接し護送されて文久二（一八六二）年閏八月十四日伊延港に着岸、但牢舎の成るのを待つ為なお船牢に在って十六日上陸
昭和三十八年十一月

と刻まれている。

南洲神社

明治三十四年西郷神社を造営、大正の初めごろ南洲神社に改称、全国五か所にある南洲神社のうち、早いうちに建立した。資金の一部を社倉から支出した。西郷隆盛立像は昭和五十二年鹿児島市で開催された没後百周年記念行事終了後に寄贈されたものである。

西郷南洲没後百年に当り西郷隆盛の立像をゆかりの地和泊町に贈呈します。沖永良部住民皆様の心の支柱になればこの上の喜びはありません。
南日本放送会長　畠中　秀隆
南日本放送の御厚意を尊重しこの地に敬慕する南洲翁の立像を建立します
和泊町長　武田　恵喜光
昭和五十三年八月十四日建立

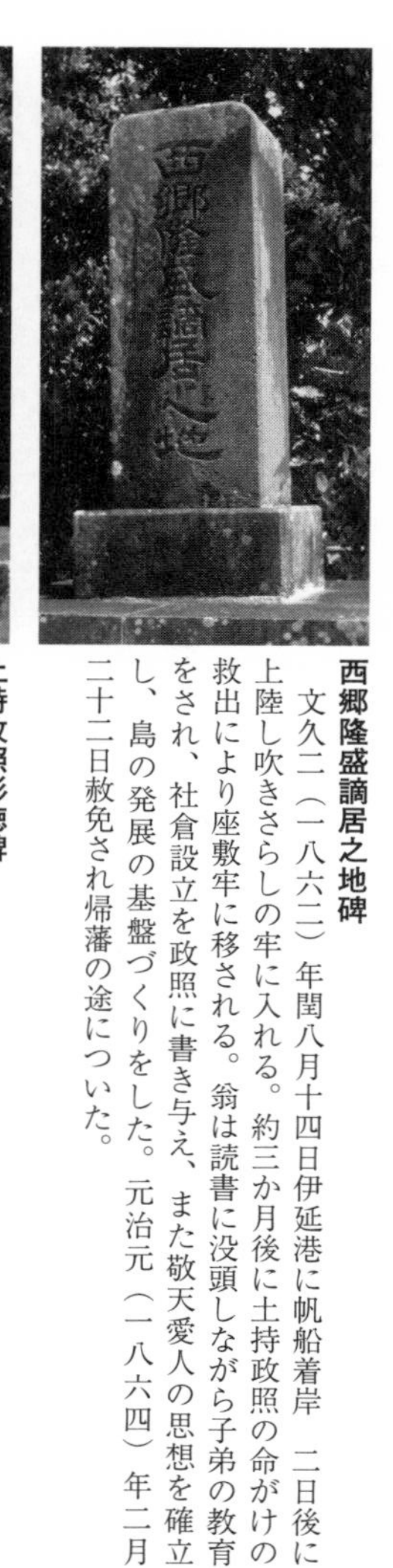

西郷隆盛謫居之地碑

文久二（一八六二）年閏八月十四日伊延港に帆船着岸　二日後に上陸し吹きさらしの牢に入れる。約三か月後に土持政照の命がけの救出により座敷牢に移される。翁は読書に没頭しながら子弟の教育をされ、社倉設立を政照に書き与え、また敬天愛人の思想を確立し、島の発展の基盤づくりをした。元治元（一八六四）年二月二十二日赦免され帰藩の途についた。

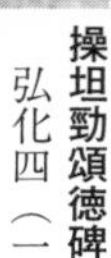

土持政照彰徳碑

代官土持叶之丞綱政と島妻鶴との長男　天保五年十一月四日生　西郷牢居中は間切横目として活躍、吹きさらし牢の西郷を命がけで救出、義兄弟の契りを結ぶ、明治三年与人として社倉創立に尽力、明治五年上京し砂糖負債返納を翁に嘆願　明治二十年初代和泊方戸長　明治三十五年十二月四日　六十九歳死去明治三十九年彰徳碑建立

操坦勁頌徳碑

弘化四（一八四七）年与人坦栽と加弥の長男として生まれる　西郷牢居中南洲塾で指導を受ける。明治八年方医学生として鹿児島へ留学派遣　明治十三年戸長　明治十五年初代知名方戸長　明治二十七年二代和泊方戸長　明治四十一年初代知名村長　大正十二年十月十四日七十七歳死去　大正十五年頌徳碑建立

西郷南洲記念館
南洲翁の遺墨、遺品等が展示されています。
（平成23年７月完成）

敬天愛人発祥の地碑
文久２（1862）年沖永良部島へ流罪となり、１年６か月過酷な牢屋ぐらしを送りましたが、その間、天地自然の理を悟り、敬天愛人の大思想を完成させました。これが本島発展の礎をなしています。
和泊西郷南洲顕彰会創立25周年記念として平成15年２月建立。

川口雪篷謫居の地
不敬の罪に問われ、その連座により嘉永四（1851）年に遠島となり西原村に居住して子弟に習字を教えた。赦免後は西郷家の執事となり、西郷没後は遺族の面倒をみて、明治23年、73歳で死去した。

※以上の写真などは和泊西郷南洲記念館　宗淳氏のご協力を頂きました。

第三章　近代日本の夜明け（明治維新）

一、風は南風

元治元（一八六四）年二月二十三日昼ごろ龍郷村に着いた西郷は、最愛の妻愛加那とそれに二人の子どもと三泊四日の楽しい時間を過ごします。徳之島で親子が北と南に別れてから一年半ぶりの再会でした。菊次郎は、父吉之助を見るなり、広い父の胸に飛び込んできます。菊子は恥ずかしそうに、母に促されて父の膝に乗り、時折顔を上げて、可愛い手で父のあごひげをさすっています。西郷は、ただ笑みを浮かべて、二人の子どもをしっかり抱きしめて離そうとしません。この光景を側で見ながら愛加那は涙が出るのを我慢しているようでした。

夕方になると、村人たちが大勢、愛加那の家へやってきて、吉井や従道らも交えてにぎやかな宴が開かれました。

運命とは皮肉なもので、後年、菊次郎が九歳、菊子は十四歳になると鹿児島の西郷家へひきとられていきます。残された母愛加那は、生涯二人の子どもの行く末を案じながら六十六歳でこの世を去ります。「女は結婚しても島を離れることは許されない」という無言の掟（おきて）を承知の上での西郷との結婚でしたから。

愛加那

龍郷を出航した胡蝶丸は、喜界島に寄港し、同志の村田新八を同乗させ、一路鹿児島へ向かいます。西郷は、船中で徳之島や沖永良部島でのことを、なつかしく思い出していました。

「私は、この年になるまで二度も遠島になった話は聞いたことがない。西郷様、あなたは二度目というではありませんか、二度あることは三度あると昔から言われています。今度こそ心を入れかえて立派なお侍さんにおなりなさい」との徳之島の老婆の有難いお言葉。沖永良部島では、命をかけて瀕死状態の私を、牢から救出してくれた土持政照など、南海の孤島で暮らす人々の情愛の深さにしみじみと感謝していました。西郷自らも出会いを大事にする島の人々に感化され敬天愛人の思想に目覚め、生まれ変わって帰れる喜びを嚙みしめながら、夢は南風に乗って日本の大地を目ざして飛翔していきます。

桜島と錦江湾

久し振りに見る桜島は噴煙を空高く舞い上げて歓迎してくれ、また、勇気を与えてくれました。

鹿児島に到着すると、すぐさま今は亡き主君斉彬公の墓前に参り、帰郷報告と恩返しの決意を誓いました。そして藩主忠義公より軍賦役（軍事司令官）と諸藩応接掛を命じられました。ほっとする間もなく、京都へ上ることになりました。

二、禁門の変と西郷隆盛

元治元年三月中旬、西郷は京都に到着し、久光公や幼友達大久保利通などと会い、藩内情勢や御所警護について話を聞きます。それによると、京都は御所を巡って尊皇攘夷派と公武合体派の対立が激化しており、特に、尊皇攘夷派の長州の動きが先鋭化しているということでした。御所内の長州寄りの七卿が退去を命じられ、これにより会津、薩摩、越前、桑名などの幕府側（公武合体派）と長州藩との間には処々でいさかいが絶えません。

七月になると御所警護を追われた長州兵は、再び御所内突入を目指し三門から勇猛果敢に攻めていきます。乾門を守っていた薩摩軍は西郷の陣頭指揮のもと、禁門にかけつけ交戦して撃退します。会津藩が守りを固めていた禁門（蛤御門）を打ち破り洛中突破に出させ、勝負を決めました。捕虜となった長州兵を薩摩藩邸に連行し衣服や食料を与え丁重にあつかい、その後、長州に送り帰したという。この戦いにより京都の市内は二日間にわたって火災となり、民家四万戸が焼失しました。西郷は流弾を受け足に軽傷を負いましたが、それでも勇敢に指揮を執り「薩摩に西郷あり」の名声を天下にとどろかせました。この戦いを禁門の変（蛤御門の変）と言います。

この禁門の変では、幕府側の勝利になりましたが、この時、西郷は幕府の軍艦奉行勝海舟とその弟子坂本龍馬と、長州攻めや公武合体について語り合う機会を得ました。勝は「現在の幕府は、その権限と責任がどこにあるのか、全くわからない。これからは雄藩が力を合わせて国を動かす時だ」と幕府の要人でありながら内輪を批判している。そうした勝の心の広さと人物に西郷は惚れていきます。同年八月に入ると、幕府は禁門の変の勢いに乗じて、更に長州攻めを決定します。総督に徳川慶勝、総参謀に西郷を任命します。西郷は、勝の心中を察しており、雄藩なる長州と戦わずして勝つ方法を模索していました。それには長州は、自分たちが朝廷に手向かった禁門の変のことを謝罪し指揮した家老たちを長州自ら処分するという方法でした。

そのために、西郷は自ら長州へ出向き誠意をもって説得に努めました。長州は敵の総参謀がひとりで乗り込んできたことの重大さや国内の戦いの空しさに同調し、これを受け入れ、これによって幕府は戦わずして勝つことになりました。これが第一次長州征伐となりました。長州では更にアメリカ・フランス・オランダ及びイギリスの四国艦隊の報復攻撃を受け下関は壊滅状態となっていました。（長州は禁門の変以前に下関海峡を通過するアメリカ、フランス等の船を砲撃し、攘夷を力で誇示していたのでした。）

三、大政奉還

幕府は、禁門の変、第一次長州征伐で勝利したことから、自分たちが座して命ずれば長州藩は服従するかのような錯覚にまでなっていました。そこで、第二次の長州征伐も安心感を持って計画し命令を発したのです。対する長州藩は続く敗戦状況を顧みて、尊皇攘夷から、〝倒幕〟へと藩論を統一していきます。また坂本龍馬らを介して薩長同盟を結び、軍事上の協力体制ができていました。薩摩は幕府側から離れていったのです。

慶応二（一八六六）年六月、幕府は勅許を得ないまま、第二次長州征伐を決行したのです。薩摩は参戦しませんでした。

迎え討つ長州は、士気に燃え、新式の武器を揃え、兵術もすぐれており、到る所で連戦連勝を果していきます。幕府軍は苦戦を強いられる中、将軍徳川家茂が大坂城で病死します。後見役の徳川慶喜は、権威回復を目指し、幕臣たちの再起を促しますが、長州軍の攻勢には堪えきれません。

ついに、幕府は将軍の死を口実に休戦に切り換え、その交渉を謹慎中の勝海舟に一任します。長州もこれに応じ、幕府軍は撤退し、長州軍は追撃しないという協定が結ばれました。

この長州征伐が幕府の大敗に終わったことで、各地の討幕派の勢いは日に日に高まっていきます。坂本龍馬の出身の土佐藩では、幕府の終焉（しゅうえん）の近いことを察し、幕府に対して大政奉還の建白書を提出します。将軍徳川慶喜は建白書を真摯（しんし）に受け止め、慶応三（一八六七）年十月十四日、ついに天皇に政権返上を奉請（ほうせい）しました。朝廷は、翌十五日この上奏（じょうそう）を許す旨の詔勅（しょうちょく）を下されました。

これにより、徳川家康が慶長八（一六〇三）年に築いた江戸幕府は、二百六十四年の歴史の幕を閉じることになりました。日本はこの大政奉還により、長年の武家中心の封建社会から自由で四民平等の近代国家へと脱皮していくことになり、国の政治は徳川幕府から天皇へ返還されることになりました。明治維新の足音も高く響き渡っていきます。

【大政奉還の背景】

嘉永六（一八五三）年アメリカ東インド艦隊司令長官ペリーが浦賀に入港します。以来、幕府はペリーの要求により日米和親条約、続いて修好通商条約を結びます。これにより日本は下田・箱館の二港を開港し水や食料を提供、更に新潟、横浜等五港を開港して自由貿易をおし進めていきます。毛織物、武器等の輸入、生糸・茶の輸出などが盛んになりますが、その関税などは当事国に委ねられ、また、犯罪を犯した外国人の裁判権は、その国の法律によることになります。これらの不平等条約適用によって日本の物価は急上昇し、庶民の生活は著しく苦しくなっていきます。これに不満をつのらせていた薩摩と長州は同盟して倒幕に乗り出します。将軍徳川慶喜は不満爆発を恐れて政権の座を朝廷に返上します。これを大政奉還と言います。しかし権威にこだわる東北・北陸諸藩の旧幕府軍は激しく抵抗し、朝敵とされながらも朝廷軍と戦うことになります。ペリー来航後十五年が過ぎていました。

南洲翁遺訓十七

正道を踏み国を以て斃るるの精神無くば、外国交際は全かる可からず。彼の強大に畏縮し、円滑を主として、曲げて彼の意に順従する時は、軽侮を招き、好親却って破れ、終に彼の制を受くるに至らん。

（解釈）　正しい道を踏み国を賭して、倒れてもやるという精神がないと外国との交際は全うすることはできない。外国の強大に恐れ、ちぢこまり、ただ円滑にこれを納めることを主眼にして、自国の真意を曲げてまで外国のいうままに従うことは、あなどりを受け、親しい交わりが却って破れ、しまいには外国に制圧されるに至るであろう。

四、戊辰戦争（維新戦争）と西郷隆盛

大政奉還後、朝廷は朝議を経て新政府の母体となる総裁・議定・参与の三職を決定し、王政復古の大号令を天下に発表します。更に公家岩倉具視を中心に尾張、福井、広島、土佐、薩摩の首脳を集め、小御所会議を開き、徳川の辞官、納地について話し合いがなされました。

徳川慶喜は、この報を大坂城で聞き、ないがしろにされたことに激高し、薩長討伐に乗り出します。慶応四年（一八六八）一月二日慶喜は一万五千人の大軍を率いて京都を目ざします。

対する薩長軍は、京都鳥羽口で旧幕府軍に砲火を浴びせ、続く伏見口でも戦闘は開始され、戊辰戦争の火蓋が切られました。すでに天皇は薩長等の手中にあり、旧幕府軍は「錦の御旗」の前に朝敵とされ、腰砕けとなっていきます。

また、旧幕府軍に名を連ねていた各藩も次々と朝廷軍に寝返りしていきます。総大将徳川慶喜は、戦う幕臣たちを残したまま江戸へ逃げ帰る始末でした。こうして、鳥羽・伏見の戦いは朝廷軍の旺盛な士気、西郷のすぐれた軍略によって勝利をおさめることができました。

西郷・勝会談

慶応四年二月、西郷は朝廷軍総参謀に任じられ、江戸に向け進撃を続けます。江戸に逃げ帰った慶喜は、旧幕府総裁に勝海舟を任命し、戦いの結末を一任します。自らは上野寛永寺にて恭順の意を示しました。勝は、無益な戦いを避け、江戸市民の生命と財産を守り、数万人の旧幕臣の生活を保障させるため、西郷との会談を希望していました。徳川に嫁いだ天璋院（家定夫人）と和宮（家茂夫人）からは、慶喜の助命嘆願と徳川氏存続の請願が大総督にすでに提出されていました。

勝の申し出で、西郷との会談は、二度行われました。両雄の会談は肝胆相照らす旧知の仲で和やかなうちに終りました。

江戸城は三月十五日の総攻撃の中止により戦禍を免れ、四月に正式に無血開城として朝廷軍に引き渡されます。西郷は勝との会談後京都へ上って、大総督に報告し、三職会議を開いて諸報告をされるなど、わずか三週間の活躍は超人的努力をしたことになります。

五、荘内藩と西郷隆盛

徳川の本陣江戸城は、西郷・勝両雄の見事な識見と誠実な会談により、無血で朝廷に明け渡すことになりましたが、恩義をかけられてきた東北・北陸の諸藩は、なおも抵抗し、徳川の再起に望みをかけます。朝廷は日本の近代化を進めるには統一した国づくりがどうしても必要でした。薩摩、長州を中心とした朝廷軍は一進一退の激戦を強いられ、大きな犠牲を伴いました。西郷の弟吉次郎は、「今度は私も力になりたい」と参戦を申し出て、越後長岡戦に加わっていましたが、戦況は思わしくなく戦死してしまいました。西郷はこれまで、吉次郎が家事に専念してくれたおかげで、国事に携わることができたのであり、そのことをいつも感謝していましたが、戦死の報に接し、深く嘆き悲しみ、頭髪を剃って丸刈りになり、弟の死を悼んだそうです。

東北・北陸の各藩は、次々に陥落していく中、荘内藩は頑強で決死の勢いで挑んできます。しかし遂に力尽きて降伏します。

降伏式は、藩校致道館講堂で行われました。薩摩藩参謀黒田清隆は数名の兵士を伴い講堂に入ります。講堂内には武装したままの藩士一同がかたずを呑んで待ち構えています。高座に座った黒田は、下座に端坐している荘内藩主酒井忠篤（十六歳）に降伏文書を読み上げ、条件を言い渡しました。「藩公は菩提寺にて休養し、王政復古の大道を踏み行うべきこと、藩士一同は謹慎とし佩刀は武士の礼儀として許されること。」黒田は読み終わると、藩主忠篤公の手を取って高座に案内し、自分は下座に正座して「先程は役目がら失礼しました。これからは藩公の礼をもってご待遇いたします」と両手をつきました。藩士たちは厳しい報復があるものと覚悟していましたが、黒田の寛大な処置に感激しました。それというのも、一年前に江戸の薩摩藩邸を焼き打ちにしたのは荘内藩であったからです。黒田の一挙一動が、すべて西郷の命によるものと知って、荘内藩の人々は西郷の人徳に感謝と尊敬の念を抱いたのでした。

以来、荘内藩の人々は西郷の徳を敬慕し、明治三年から明治九年まで、藩主酒井忠篤、家老菅実秀ほか百名余りの人々がはるばる鹿児島を訪れて、西郷の教えを受けています。

その後、教えを受けた藩士たちは菅の命により、西郷の教えを互いに復唱し「南洲翁遺訓」としてまとめました。

明治二十二（一八八九）年南洲翁遺訓集として編集発行し、翌年、荘内藩士たちが全国行脚して配布して廻ったということです。本書には、南洲翁遺訓総則五十三則のうち六則を掲載させてもらいました。

六、西郷政権と西郷隆盛の質素な私生活

鳥羽・伏見の戦いで火蓋をきった戊辰戦争は、江戸、東北・北陸そして箱館まで、苦戦の末、朝廷軍の勝利で終わりました。少数派であった薩摩・長州がよく連携して乗り切れたものだと思います。西郷の私欲を捨てた誠実、度量そして勇気、すなわち敬天愛人の信条こそ勝利の真髄と言えましょう。

その後、西郷は明治政府の出仕を断り、郷里鹿児島へ帰って温泉治療をしながら、犬

を連れて山歩きを楽しんでいました。

明治二年、西郷は新政府より論功行賞として最高の賞典禄二千石を贈られます。そして、正三位に叙せられましたが、藩主などよりも上位なので情義に反するとして、これを辞退しました。この年、明治政府は版籍奉還（領土と人民を天皇に返す）を実行します。あわせて明治維新の最大の課題は、藩を廃し、藩主も藩士もなくすることでした。それによってすべての国民が、自由で平等となり、近代国家をつくる基本になるからです。いわゆる廃藩置県であります。これには全国の藩主や武士たちの抵抗は必至で、容易なことでは実行できません。そこで明治政府は再三再四実行力のある西郷の出仕を要請しますが断り続けます。明治天皇は遂に勅使を派遣し、西郷の上京を命ずることになりました。西郷の人望と力量に待つほかなかったからです。

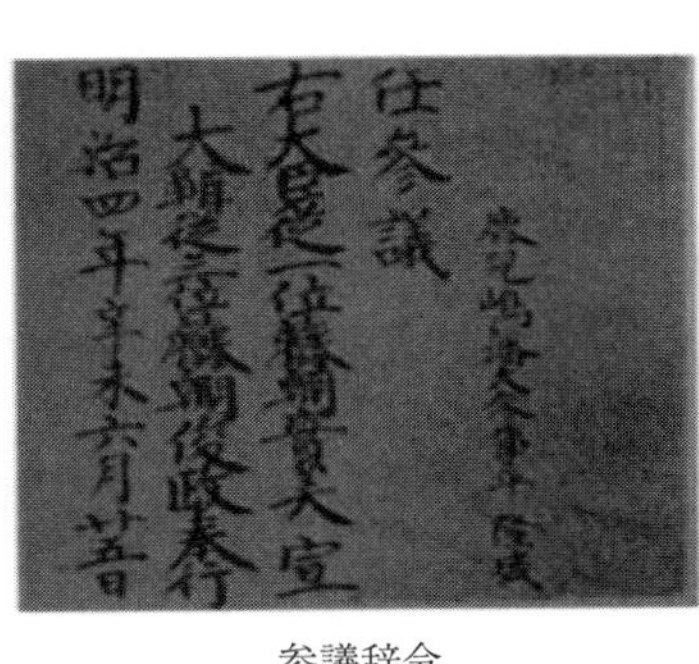
鹿児島藩大参事 [illegible]
任参議
右大臣従一位藤原朝臣[illegible]宣
大納言[illegible]奉行
明治四年辛未六月[illegible]

参議辞令

明治四年六月、西郷は筆頭参議に就任し、実力者等を登用し、廃藩置県を断行します。以来郵便局、銀行、鉄道の事業創設、義務教育の学制改革、地租税改革、警察制度、徴兵制度等、次々に近代化の波に乗って整備していきます。

また、天皇の教育係に山岡鉄太郎（鉄舟）、吉井友実を任命し、剛健な天皇になってもらうための策を講じたのです。

その年の十一月、岩倉具視を団長として、大久保利通ら一行四十八名の欧米視察団が派遣されました。名目は、幕政時代に結ばれた不平等条約の改正交渉と、文物調査でした。西郷らに留守を任せた。「廃藩置県」の重大問題を実施したばかりで、情勢不安な時期の派遣でありました。

西郷の私生活はどんなだったでしょうか。参議としての報酬は月五百円（現在の百五十万円）でした。これだけの報酬だったら、他の高官たちのように、豪邸に住み、贅沢な生活ができたはずなのに、西郷は、日本橋小網町の旧姫路藩の蔵屋敷を月三円で借り、二部屋の他に応接間と熊吉らの一部屋があるだけでした。生活費は二十円ぐらいで足りました。残りは郷里からの学生や若者たちが来て必要なだけ持ち帰り、なお余りは造士館へ寄付していました。役所へは徒歩で通勤し、昼の食事は竹の皮で包んだにぎり飯かソバですまし、着物は薩摩絣一枚のみでした。実に外見をはばからず、質素な私生活で三年間を過ごしました。西郷の人気の秘訣はこうした庶民的な生活にもあったのでした。

七、征韓論（せいかんろん）と西南の役

明治六年五月、朝鮮との間に外交上の問題が起きました。朝鮮へ送った公文書が誤解され、日本製品の輸入禁止や日本居留民の強制送還など不穏（ふおん）な動きが持ち上がってきました。新政府は朝鮮との交渉を進めようとしますが、うまくいきません。こうした中、武力で朝鮮に開国を迫る主張即ち征韓論が新政府内でも高まってきました。そこで閣議を開き、いったん朝鮮使節として西郷の派遣を決定しました。太政（だじょう）大臣三条実美（さねとみ）は、欧米使節団の帰国を待って天皇の裁可を得るからと派遣を先延ばしにしました。十月視察団が帰国すると、再度閣議が開かれ、西郷の朝鮮使節派遣が決定されました。ところが、三条は高熱を出し、人事不省に陥（おちい）り岩倉が太政大臣代理として天皇に奏上することになりました。

岩倉は奏上の時、朝鮮使節派遣決定と合わせて、私見（大久保らの画策した派遣中止が望ましい）も奏上したので、西郷派遣は無期延期となりました。西郷はこの時すべての職を辞し、位階返上を申し出ます。岩倉は慰留しますが、西郷の辞任はあっさりしたものでした。続いて副島種臣（そえじまたねおみ）、板垣退助、江藤新平らも参議を辞任し、また、多くの政府高官、近衛武官など西郷を敬慕する六百余名が政府を去りました。西郷の陸軍大将はそのままとされま

すが、それは兵隊の動揺を防止するための措置でした。

西郷は鹿児島に帰る前日、大久保を訪ね、帰郷の挨拶をしました。

大久保はまともに返事をしません。見送りもしませんでした。竹馬（ちくば）の友として、長年国のために働いてきた二人の最後の別れとなりました。

この朝鮮派遣問題が引き金となり、後年西南の役へと発展していくことになります。

西郷は鹿児島へ帰ると贈られた賞典禄で賞典学校、私学校を開校し、共に帰郷した官吏を中心に、維新戦争で倒れた家庭の子弟を優先的に入学させます。生徒数は毎年増えて明治九年ごろには本校分校合わせて三万人にも達しました。また、寺山高原に吉野開墾社を創設し、昼は農耕、夜は学問と、芋飯を常食としながら、自主自立の理想郷作りに情熱を傾けています。西郷も生徒と起居を共にし肥料桶をかつぎ鍬（くわ）をふるいます。


明治六年十月、西郷などが政府を去った後、異常な早さで岩倉・大久保を中心とした新政府が誕生しました。新政府は地租改正をはじめ新制度を次々に導入していきます。明治七年になると、これに反対して各地で反乱がおきます。佐賀、福岡、熊本、山口などで気勢を上げ政府を苦しめていきます。政府は鹿児島の西郷や私学校の動きも気が気でなりません。

明治十年二月一日、西郷は大隅半島にある小根占（こねじめ）というところで犬を連れて狩りに来ていました。

「ちょっ、しもた。」

西郷は悲痛な叫び声を出し、知らせに来た弟小兵衛（こべえ）の顔を見て膝を強く叩いた。「政府軍が、草牟田（そうむた）の弾薬庫から弾薬を持ち出し船に運び入れようとしているのを私学校生に見つかり、奪おうとして町中は騒然となっています」と小兵衛は、声をふるわせて報告したのでした。西郷は黙って、大きな目で時折、小兵衛を見つめるのでした。

鹿児島にある弾薬兵器は草牟田と磯、上ノ原の三か所に保管されており、県庁が管理を任されていました。このとき政府軍は県庁に事前に連絡せず、しかも夜間に誰知れず弾薬を持ち出そうとして、私学校の生徒と奪い合いになってしまったというのです。

政府は以前から密偵（みってい）を鹿児島にもぐりこませ、西郷暗殺計画や私学校の動向などに神経を尖（とが）らせていました。危急を感じた政府が早めに弾薬や兵器の大坂移送を考えての今回の事件でした。

西郷が小根占から鹿児島へ戻ったのは二日後のことでした。事件の一部始終を聞き、今すべきことは『西郷暗殺や密偵について政府に尋問するほか道はない』と判断し、「おいどんの体をおまえらにあずけもそう」と言われ、万事は決し、気勢を上げ東京を目指すことになったのです。初めは千三百人の私学校だけの隊編成を考えていましたが、県内の元士族たちがかけつけ、続いて九州各地からも西郷の人望を慕い、次々と加わり、たちまち三万人に達しました。中には「西郷先生に一日接すれば一日の愛が生じ、三日接すれば三日の愛が生まれる」と言った大分の増田宋太郎が中津隊を編成して加わっていました。

明治十年二月十七日鹿児島は五十年来の大雪が降り続いていました。西郷は陸軍大将の略服姿で磯街道を東進していました。

一方の政府軍は陸軍中将山縣有朋、海軍中将川村純義の二人を征討参謀とし大坂に総督本営が置かれました。薩軍が鹿児島を出発したことを察知して政府は熊本に援軍を送っていたのでした。

二月二十一日午前一時の深夜、熊本まで後八キロメートルという所で別府晋介の率いる薩軍の先鋒隊が急襲されたのである。これに気づいた薩軍は逆襲に転じ政府軍を退却させました。これが西南の役の火蓋を切ったことになりました。西郷は鹿児島を出る時「自分の方から絶対発砲するな」と指示していたので、政府軍から戦いを挑んできたことは明らかであります。熊本城での攻防戦は最初の激戦となり、双方とも多大な犠牲を伴うことになりました。兵力・武器・弾薬にすぐれた政府軍を薩軍は抜刀隊（ばっとうたい）などで苦しめましたが、八代方面に上陸した政府軍に背後を衝（つ）かれ、大隊長篠原国幹（くにもと）、西郷の弟小兵衛ら多数の勇士を失うことになりました。

雨の田原坂戦は、十七日間に及び、劣勢の薩軍は、八代、人吉、宮崎、そして延岡と敗走するしかなかったのです。

延岡を目指して北上した薩軍は和田峠を拠点にして反撃を試みるが、ここもすでに、政府軍に包囲されていました。これまで各隊長に指揮を任せてきた西郷は、最後になって全軍に解散命令を布告します。「我が軍は、今や窮地に追い込まれました。この際、降伏するもよし、死するもよし、皆、それぞれの自由な意志に任せる」というものでした。

この布告の後、皆涙を流し、残念な思いで、政府軍に投降（とうこう）する者四千人、残兵は僅か五百人となり、西郷軍の名のもとに故郷を目ざす虎豹（こひょう）の群となってしまいました。西郷は、熊本城戦で右足に被弾し、それでも父（西郷）についてきた愛加那との子菊次郎に、以後

最後の激戦地・故山城山

は投降して治療をするようにと熊吉に依頼しました。そして、本営にしていた児玉邸の庭で陸軍大将の略服や重要書類を焼却しました。連れてきた二匹の犬に別れを告げて放してやりました。

わずか、五百人となった西郷軍は、包囲されている可愛岳（えのだけ）を脱出し、道なき岩石だらけの山肌をよじ登りようやく山頂に到着することができました。途中政府軍の攻撃を避けながら、山、川、谷を這（は）いずり、助け合いながら一路鹿児島を目指します。行く先々では村人たちの心あたたまる援助や励ましを受けながら、九月一日遂に鹿児島吉田村入りを果しました。百九十九日ぶりに故郷へ戻ってきました。西郷帰ると聞いて鹿児島市内外とも俄（にわ）かに活気づき城山入りの快挙に沸きました。民間からは食料や衣類、兵器などを届けようとしますが、いずれも政府軍に取り上げられ、城山入りが出来たのはほんのわずかでした。
九月四日には、西郷軍抜刀隊七十人が、政府の拠点米蔵（現市役所当たり）を襲撃しますが、奮戦の末鎮圧されます。中に中津隊隊長の増田宋太郎がいました。彼は解散布告があった時、自分の隊員たちに「君たちは若い、故郷へ帰って、みんなのために働け、私は最後まで西郷先生についていく」と言って別れ別れになったのでした。

城山はもはや五万八千人の政府軍に包囲され、蟻の這い出る隙間もないほどになっています。西郷軍内では、西郷の助命嘆願が話し合われていました。九月十三日河野主一郎と山野田一輔が政府軍参謀川村純義に面会し、西郷の助命を嘆願します。「今となっては致し方ない、政府軍は明日夜明けとともに総攻撃することになっている。帰ったら西郷に言ってくれ、若し何かこの私に言いたいことがあるならば本日午後五時までに本陣に来い」と実に冷たい言い方をされました。山野田は、会談の顚末を西郷に報告しますと、西郷は決然として「回答の要はない」と言われました。これを聞いて全将兵は決死の覚悟をしました。

その夜、城山では西郷を囲んで決別の宴が催されました。酒を酌み交わし歌い、ある者は詩を吟じて、これまでの二百余日の悪戦苦闘の日々を忘れたかのように互いの健闘を賛えて、恰も古戦場を思わせる風でした。空には中秋の名月が雲間に見え隠れしながら淡い光を放ち、政府軍側からは、「君が代」（フェントン作曲）の儀礼演奏のメロディーが流れてきました。敵味方の別なく別れを惜しむ大戦前夜の悲哀に満ちた光景でした。フェントンはイギリス人で明治二年から薩摩藩の要請を受け軍楽隊や宮内省楽部を指導しています。君が代は現行の国歌と歌詞は同じですがメロディーは西洋音階によるものでした。

明治十年九月二十四日午前三時五十五分、三発の号砲を合図に政府軍の総攻撃が始まりました。政府軍は市内各方面から城山めがけて殺到、丘上に迫り銃火を集中させます。そして本陣の岩崎谷へ砲火を浴びせます。西郷は白襦袢の上に筒袖の着物、短い袴、草鞋、白い兵子帯に小刀の姿で洞窟を出られ数人の兵士に付き添われ岩崎谷口へ向かって歩き始めます。弾丸は、雨あられのように四方八方から飛んできます。三百メートルぐらい下ったところで、西郷は肩と股を射られました。もう歩けなくなってしまいました。

「晋どん、晋どん、もうここらでよか」と西郷は別府晋介に言いました。

西郷は言い終わると地面に座し襟を正して両手を合わせ静かにはるか東方を拝しました。

「先生、許し給んせ」と、晋介は叫んで恩師西郷を介錯しました。

西郷の死んだことを知って、残るものは皆、決死の勢いで、弾雨の中を駆け下り、勇壮に戦って西郷に続いて死んでいきました。午前七時銃口の音は止み、戦いは終わりました。空は俄かに暗くなり雷鳴轟き、風雨激しく降り注いで戦死者の鮮血を洗い流しました。

西郷四十九歳波瀾の生涯の幕切れでした。

振り返れば、六年前西郷は筆頭参議として明治政府を立ち上げ、富国強兵の政策のもと、国や国民を守るため軍隊や警察の創設、充実に尽力しましたが、今、西南戦争においては、図らずも自ら心血を注いで育てあげたこれら一部の官僚との間に、どんなボタンのかけ違いがあったのか、敵味方になって戦う羽目になり、命を落としてしまいました。誠に悲しい出来事でした。しかしながら、西郷の生涯、信条とした敬天愛人の精神、真正直さ、礼儀正しさ、私欲を捨てて、国のため働き通した功績は〝革命的英雄西郷隆盛〟の名を時代を超えて永遠にほめ賛えられていくことでしょう。

かつての戊辰戦争で頂上会談をし、江戸市中を戦禍から守った盟友勝海舟は、この西南戦争での西郷の働

弾痕なまなましい私学校の塀

西郷軍最後の住み処

きを述懐し、次の歌を残しています。

ぬれ衣を　干さんともせず子どもらの
なすがまにまに果てし君かな

この勝にして、またこの西郷、お二人の心情が読み取れる歌でありります。

［西郷南洲先生を慕う詩］

風は南風　維新の風

一、国の礎（いしずえ）　築きたる
男一途（いちず）に　命懸け
獄の苦しみ　耐え忍び
目指す天下の　大舞台
風は南風　維新の風
吹けよ吹け吹け　都の空に

二、明治の夜明け今ぞ知る
自由と平和の世の中に
桜の花も　麗しく
敬天愛人　人の道
風は南風　維新の風
吹けよ吹け吹け　民（たみ）の胸に

三、空を見上げ　手を合わす
君の面影　偲びつつ
恩に報ゆる　西郷どん
誠尽し　突き進む
風は南風　維新の風
吹けよ吹け吹け　日本の郷（さと）に

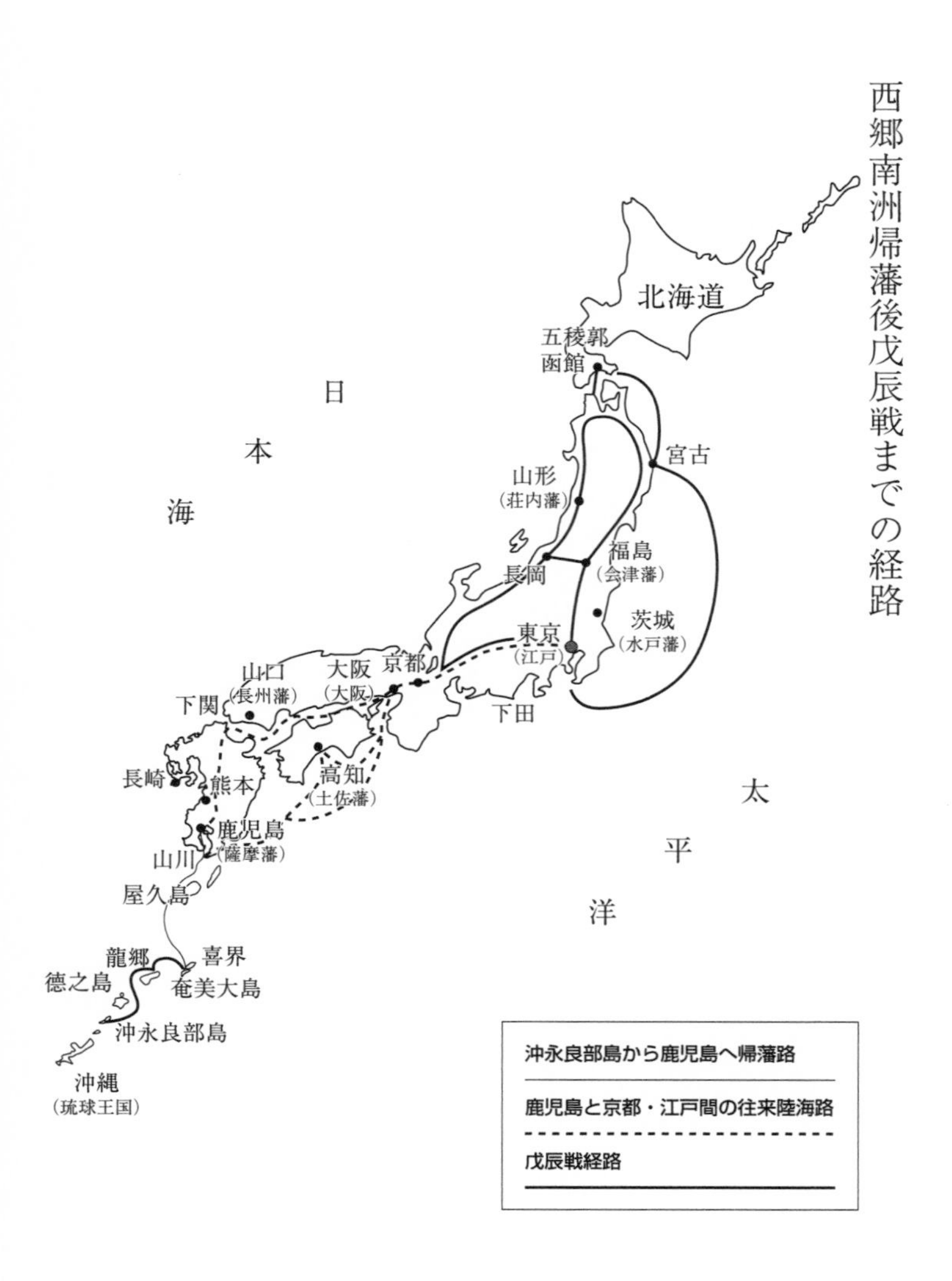
西郷南洲帰藩後戊辰戦までの経路
北海道
五稜郭
函館
日
本
海
宮古
山形
（荘内藩）
福島
（会津藩）
長岡
茨城
（水戸藩）
東京
（江戸）
京都
大阪
（大阪）
山口
（長州藩）
下関
下田
長崎
熊本
高知
（土佐藩）
鹿児島
（薩摩藩）
山川
屋久島
太
平
洋
龍郷
喜界
徳之島
奄美大島
沖永良部島
沖縄
（琉球王国）
沖永良部島から鹿児島へ帰藩路
鹿児島と京都・江戸間の往来陸海路
戊辰戦経路

西南戦争以後の年表（略史）

一八七七　明治10年9月24日　西南戦争城山で終結
山県有朋総参謀は西郷軍を丁重に検死する
一八七八　明治11年5月14日　大久保利通暗殺される（47歳）
一八八五　明治18年12月22日　伊藤博文初代首相
一八八七　明治20年　西郷菊次郎米国留学、28年台湾総督府勤務
29年宜蘭支庁長　37年京都市長
45年永野金山鉱業館長
一八八八　明治21年4月30日　黒田清隆　第二代首相
一八八九　明治22年2月11日　大日本帝国憲法発布　西郷隆盛大赦により賊名を解かれ正
三位を追贈される
一八八九　明治22年12月24日　山県有朋　第三代首相
一八九〇　明治23年　荘内藩（山形県）南洲翁遺訓初版発行全国へ配布

一八九一　明治24年5月6日　松方正義　第四代首相
一八九二　明治25年6月3日　嗣子寅太郎華族（侯爵）を授かる
一八九八　明治31年6月30日　大隈重信　第八代首相
一八九八　明治31年12月18日　東京上野の銅像除幕（高村光雲作）
一九〇一　明治34年6月2日　桂太郎　第十一代首相
一九〇二　明治35年8月27日　愛加那没（66歳）
一九〇三　明治36年　酉三没（31歳）
一九〇九　明治42年　大山菊子没（47歳）
（一九一九）　大正8年　寅太郎没（54歳）
（一九二二）　大正11年6月3日　西郷イト没（80歳）
（一九二八）　昭和3年　菊次郎没（68歳）
（一九三五）　昭和10年　午次郎没（66歳）
一九〇六　明治39年1月7日　西園寺公望　第十二代首相
一九一三　大正2年2月20日　山本権兵衛　第十六代首相
一九二七　昭和2年9月24日　西郷没後五十年祭催行

一九三七　昭和12年5月23日　鹿児島・城山麓の銅像除幕（安藤照作）

一九七七　昭和52年9月24日　西郷没後百年祭催行

＝各地の西郷南洲翁研究会の紹介＝

一般社団法人　薩摩士魂の会

〒一〇七－〇〇六二　東京都港区南青山一－一五－一四
㈱豊建築事務所内
電話　〇三－五七八六－五七八八

代表理事　森園　安男
幹事長　橋口　一徳

一、幕末明治維新の人物、史実の研究
二、研究成果の発表
三、志を共有する全国の方々との交流、訪問

薩摩士魂の始祖・島津日新齋　竹田神社

四、書籍等の販売

公益財団法人　荘内南洲会

〒九九八―〇〇五五　山形県酒田市飯森山二―三〇四―一〇

電話　〇二三四―三一―二三六四

理事長　水野　貞吉

常任理事　阿曽　昇

一、人間学講座　月一回

二、教学と歴史の研修と研修旅行

三、「敬天」の発行

四、「南洲翁遺訓」贈呈版の無償頒布

南洲翁と荘内藩家老　菅　実秀翁
「徳の交わり」像

公益財団法人　西郷南洲顕彰会

〒八九二-〇八五一　鹿児島市上竜尾町二-一
電話　〇九九-二四七-一一〇〇

代表理事　桂　久昭
常務理事　徳永　和喜

一、南洲遺訓学習会　毎月
二、各種講座・講演会開催
三、史跡巡り・研修旅行
四、「敬天愛人」発行

西郷どんの遠行（せごどんのえんこ）

和泊西郷南洲顕彰会

〒八九一－九一一二　鹿児島県大島郡和泊町和泊一〇

（和泊町中央公民館内）

電話　〇九九七－九二－〇二九〇

会　長　逆瀬川　勝久

事務局長　先　田　資秀

一、講演会の開催

二、ゆかりの地訪問研修

三、学校教育への学習支援

四、書籍の販売

顕彰会創設記念講演会

講師　京セラ名誉会長　稲盛　和夫氏

西郷隆盛に学ぶ「敬天愛人フォーラム21」

〒一〇一－〇〇四七　東京都千代田区内神田三－一八－五
神多ビル四階
電話　〇三－三二五二－三一五三

代表世話役　内　弘志

一、「西郷隆盛に学ぶ」勉強会開催
二、ゆかりの地の研修旅行
三、西郷隆盛・勝海舟の慰霊祭催行
四、上野公園西郷銅像周辺の清掃及び生誕祭

毎月第２日曜　西郷銅像周辺の清掃作業実施

参考

西郷隆盛（王道の巻）　海音寺潮五郎
鹿児島縣史　鹿児島県
鹿児島大百科事典　南日本新聞社
南洲翁遺訓　（財）荘内南洲会
西郷隆盛（その生涯）　東郷　實晴
西郷隆盛　奥　　徹
和泊町誌　和泊町編集委員会
知名町誌　知名町編纂委員会
流謫の南洲翁　土持綱義
西郷隆盛　（財）鹿児島育英財団
嶋の南洲先生　安藤　佳翠
西郷隆盛と土持正照　玉起　寿芳
国にも金にも嵌まらず上下　鮫島志芽太
大西郷の流謫とその余徳　武田恵喜光
西郷隆盛　本部廣哲
大西郷全集　平凡社
西郷隆盛　安藤　英男
薩摩武士道　薩摩士魂の会
西郷南洲先生詩集　（財）西郷南洲顕彰会
西郷隆盛年譜　山田尚二

おわりに

本書は西郷隆盛（南洲翁）の波瀾の後半生について述べてきました。南洲翁が、なぜ革命的英雄として称賛されるかと問うならば、それは、二百六十四年続いた江戸幕府を打倒し、天皇親政の国家体制を築きあげたことであると明快に答えることができると思います。これまで誰もが成し得なかったことを、同志と共にこの偉業を、実現することが出来たからであります。

南洲翁は国を救いたいという一念から正道を踏み、幾多の困難を克服して明治維新をやり遂げました。〝敬天愛人〟を常に至上の銘として生きて来たからこそであります。

私たちは、南洲翁の敬天愛人の精神に思いを馳せながら温故知新の歴史に学び、人間愛の絆を一層強固なものにして誰もが住みやすい世の中を目指して努力を続けなければならないと思います。本書がその一助となることを願って止みません。
最後に、本書の発行にご尽力くださいました株式会社国書刊行会様及び関係者の皆様に心より感謝申し上げます。

著者　竿田　富夫
英訳　竿田　豊

令和三（二〇二一）年二月

Segodon and the Soul of the Meiji Restoration

The Birthplace of "Revere Heaven, Love People" -Okinoerabu-jima Island-

Land and Sea Route (Takamori SAIGO took)

D = DOMAIN

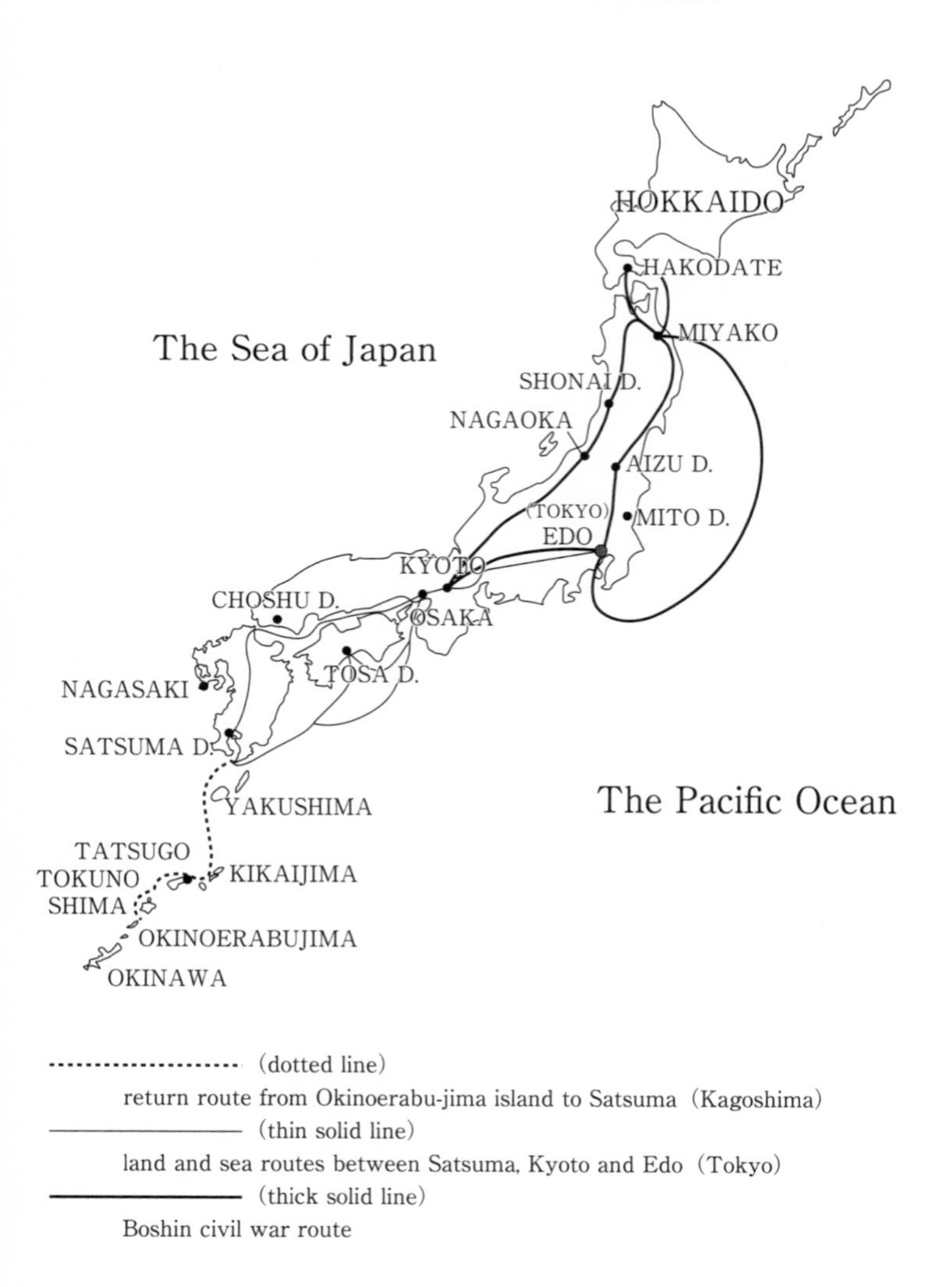

-------------------- (dotted line)

return route from Okinoerabu-jima island to Satsuma (Kagoshima)

———————— (thin solid line)

land and sea routes between Satsuma, Kyoto and Edo (Tokyo)

━━━━━━━━ (thick solid line)

Boshin civil war route

Content (s)

Introduction

Takamori SAIGO, a revolutionary hero, who led the Meiji Restoration (often called "the dawn of modern Japan,") is admired by people all over the world for his great accomplishments in Japan's modernization.

In August, 1862, he was declared a criminal and exiled onto the small island of *Okinoerabu-jima*, located between *Kyūshū* and *Okinawa* in the southern sea. He was confined in a small prison there for one and a half years until 1864. When he was released, four years were left until the Meiji Restoration.

His life there was unimaginably hard. He could have proved his innocence by taking his own life. However, he made his choice to go through the difficult ordeal sent to him by Heaven and to live a life of justice, and continued Zen meditation. Unbelievably, he found that he himself was spiritually reborn.

While in prison, he composed the following poem in Chinese:

In prison, my mind goes blank like ice, and bitterness and spiciness make me taste sweet. Terrible pains penetrate to the bone, which enables me to realize my true mind.

Nobody can see through ornate words, or falsehood. It is easy to deceive human beings, but no one can betray Heaven.

I have never done anything I might be ashamed of before Heaven, not to mention people.

SAIGO was on the verge of death, when his jailer, Masateru TSUCHIMOCHI, saved him at the risk of his own life. He was attracted by SAIGO's personality and felt that he ought to save him. The intimacy between the two was deeper than that between blood brothers, and his famous motto "Revere Heaven, Love People" is said to have been born spontaneously from each other's deep affections. In his book entitled "Takamori SAIGO" (Royal Road Volume)", Chogoro KAIONJI wrote: "It was thanks to his commitment to the ideal of "Revere Heaven, Love People" as his religious philosophy that he became able to endure all the hardships in prison life on the island of *Okinoerabu-jima*."

SAIGO was pardoned after one and a half years of imprisonment. He left the island to play a great role in Japanese history, the warm southern wind filling his cou-

rageous heart with hope.

Chapter 1 details SAIGO's struggle for life following the principle of "Revere Heaven, Love People".

Chapter 2 describes SAIGO's spiritual rebirth, regarding Heaven as his mentor.

Chapter 3 relates SAIGO's great accomplishments. It was the very spirit of the "Revere Heaven, Love People" motto that led him to success.

Particularly, the christian philosopher Kanzo UCHIMURA introduced Takamori SAIGO's great achievements in his book entitled "Representative Men of Japan"(English version), which became widely known and read by many foreign leaders, including Jhon F. Kennedy, the 35th president of the United States.

It was due mainly to his encounter with jailer Masateru TSUCHIMOCHI and the humane islanders that SAIGO, who endured a severe prison life next to death on a remote island in the southern sea, could overcome numerous difficulties and accomplish his great achievements. Therefore, this book includes an English version, because we want this fact to be known abroad too.

We were happy to receive a message from Takamitsu SAIGO, great-grandson of Takamori SAIGO. When he

visited the island for the first time in August, 2011, we had a friendly talk with him. I remember he was moved to tears when he was looking at the seated statue of Takamori SAIGO inside the prison.

At present, he is running 'STARLITE Co., Ltd.' The firm has been successful in doing business both in Japan and abroad. In addition, he is the head of the SAIGO family. He visited Okinoerabu-jima island several times to develop friendly relations with local people and donated a large amount of money for the construction of SAIGO NANSHU MEMORIAL HALL. We'd like the readers to understand his great-grandfather, Takamori SAIGO by reading his instructive message.

We would like to express our gratitude to Mr. Takamitsu SAIGO.

February, 2021

Author Tomio SAODA
English Translation Yutaka SAODA

Message from Takamitsu SAIGO, a great-grandson of Takamori SAIGO

Mr. Tomio SAODA, whom I respect, has published a book titled "Segodon and the Soul of the Meiji Restoration - The Birthplace of 'Revere Heaven, Love People': Okinoerabu-jima Island" - in Japanese and English. Born at Wadomari-cho, Okinoerabu-jima island, he took up teaching as a profession. While serving as school principal and later as superintendent of Wadomari-cho Board of Education, he has contributed greatly to music composition and to various charitable activities. I was deeply impressed to know that he taught children about the connection between SAIGO Nanshuo and the islanders, including background history, by using story telling picture cards, that he composed the big hit "Nangoku (tropical) Elegy" for Katsue TAKAISHI in 1964, and also with respect to our SAIGO family, he made a great contribution to the construction of "Wadomari-cho SAIGO Memorial Hall" which was completed in 2011. Through such relations, as Takamori SAIGO's great-grandson, I have succeeded to more than 160 years' ancestral connections, transcending time and space.

As one example, I have given a lecture at our SAIGO family get-together, "the 24th Day Meeting," as we call it held each year in Tokyo, where over 100 relatives gather on a Saturday close to September 24th, the anniversary of Takamori's death. I spoke to the members about current relations between Okinoerabu-jima island and the SAIGO

family, hoping that our relationship will continue to be enriched furthermore.

Incidentally, while taking an early morning walk, I mumble to myself, "I deeply appreciate great nature (heaven) for giving me life and a mission." This mission has been handed down from generation to generation from ancestors long before Takamori SAIGO, and I believe that each of us has executed the mission, bearing responsibility for each era. Nothing can be substituted for feeling the satisfaction of the continued eternal light and momentousness.

Books written by many writers and calligraphies left by my great-grandfather enable us to read what set him in motion and what kind of human connections set his heart ablaze during the tumultuous years of the late Edo period. Above all, though it was his fate, the occurrence in Okinoerabu-jima island was a severe reality. Realizing his own mission (Heaven's will) there, he was purified, revived, and reborn receiving blessings from tropical nature and people's warm hearts. Before he knew it, he had gained more powerful energy than he had imagined, making it possible for him to run through his circumstances as if he had been sent back to the present world. I feel that he was moved by a natural flow that exceeded his expectations after he returned to the Satsuma Domain.

As his great-grandson, in my youth, I could not follow or comprehend "Why that judgment and action in such a situation?" I still have not come up with an answer to the question, "Why did he sacrifice such a great number of young people's lives together with his?" However, the answer is no longer necessary for me because I am old

enough to be able to understand a little bit of the meaning of passionate life. At present, I have made good relationships with places where my great-grandfather left his footprints, including Okinoerabu-jima island. The spirit that he fostered together with people there is still alive to this day. Mr. SAODA has introduced to the world through his current publication the deep human connections established by Takamori SAIGO to be a great contribution. I am very grateful for his efforts, and wish to express my full gratitude to him.

When experiencing a tough time, I think the bronze statue of my great-grandfather, confined in prison at Okinoerabu-jima island. By doing so, my hardships and worries are healed. Then, I hear my great-grandfather asking me, "Takamitsu, what are you doing now for people and society?" I am awakened in surprise. I like the expression- "It is now that an infinite past meets an infinite future." I am realizing again this challenge to 'infinity' through Mr. SAODA's publication. My sincere thanks to Mr. SAODA.

Takamitsu SAIGO
President
STARLITE CO., LTD.

Chapter 1

"Revere Heaven, Love People" and Okinoerabu-jima Island

1. SAIGO- from Tokunoshima island to Okinoerabu-jima island

On leap August 14, 1862, dawn broke, and the sky in the east was gradually growing brighter and brighter. The glaring morning sun shone through the thunderclouds. In Inokawa port on the Tokunoshima island, a giant of a man was leaning against a pine tree and looking at the sky and the sea with an absent-minded air. He was concerned whether his wife, Aikana, and children could return to Tatsugo, their hometown safely, and would not get seasick on the way.

Before leaving Tokunoshima, Aikana said to him, "I wish our family could live happily on this island."

The man was Kichinosuke OSHIMA (Segodon), and he thought of his wife and children more than about himself. On that particular day, he was to be exiled to the small southern island of Okinoerabu-jima.

He was forced to make a difficult six months' journey, because he had enraged Hisamitsu, the father of the lord (daimyo) of the Satsuma Domain.

At the beginning of the year, he was in Tatsugo village, but in February he was ordered to return to Kagoshima. Then he stayed at Shimonoseki in March, Osaka and Kyoto in April, Yamakawa port in May, and Tokunoshima in July. Furthermore, in leap August of that year, he was

exiled to the island of Okinoerabu-jima. Every time he was exiled, he changed his name: Kichinosuke SAIGO, Gengo KIKUCHI, Sanuemon OSHIMA, and Kichinosuke OSHIMA. His friends called him Kichinosuke-san or his nickname, Segodon. In Amami, he was known as "Master SAIGO," his honorific title. In this paper, he is just referred to as SAIGO.

Now let's return to the beginning of the story. Around ten o'clock on that day, when he was to leave Tokunoshima island for Okinoerabu-jima island, the villagers in Inokawa gathered in the port to see him off. Among them was a 16-year-old youth named Nakayu RYU. In tears, he begged SAIGO to take him along. The youth was his disciple, whom SAIGO had taught, and who had lived under the same roof and had taken care of him for more than two months on Tokunoshima island.

Teiyoki RYU, a local police officer in charge, and an observer from Kagoshima had already gotten on board Hotokumaru ship, which was to escort SAIGO to Okinoerabu-jima island. Manbe NAKAHARA, *Daikan tsukiyaku* (assistant of the local governor in Tokunoshima) came to him with the message from *Daikan* (local governor) UEMURA: "After departure, you can leave the jail cell and feel free to spend time as you like."

He added, "Please, do as you are told".

SAIGO bid farewell to everybody and went on board the ship. Soon after the departure from Inokawa port, the rudder of the ship was turned to the south, with fair winds to fill the sails. After a while, Ryu urged SAIGO to get out of the jail cell, saying, "Please get out of the jail cell and move freely." SAIGO answered, "Thank you very

much, but I am a convict, and I cannot violate the domain's order. Please don't mind me."

He spent his time in a narrow jail cell sitting on his knees and reading books, which tells us how sincere he was. After four hours of sailing, the ship reached the port of Inobe on the northern coast of Okinoerabu-jima island. It was two o'clock in the afternoon. The ship passed safely through a narrow passage. Though narrow, it had no rocks or reefs, so since ancient times sugar carriers and passenger ships have used it.

On arriving to Inobe port, Ryu hurried to the *Daikansho* (local governor's office) in the village of Wadomari, one RI (2.4 miles) away from the port, leaving SAIGO and the observer on the ship. Meanwhile, the observer handed a letter to SAIGO. It was a secret letter from the guardian of Oshima *Daikansho*, Hisatake KATSURA. It said, "Don't engage in any rash actions, because we are sure to make every effort together with our comrades so that you will be able to return to the domain." After reading it through, he probably felt relieved and then spoke to the guardian with a smile:

"Well, I took you for an assassin who would kill me on the sea, because you were a stranger. I nestled my chest against the side of the ship so that the blade of your sword could pierce into it easily, but I was wrong. Ha, ha, ha!" He laughed away loudly.

On the other hand, Ryu, who had hurried to Wadomari Daikan's office-cum-residence, visited Gensuke TSUDURABARA and handed the domain lord's order to him. He said to him, "Mr. Daikan, it is the document regarding changing Mr. Oshima's island of exile. The ship

already arrived in Inobe port."

Daikan looked surprised at the sudden turn of events and read the document two or three times: "Confine inside an enclosure day and night under two jailers."

Ryu added, "Daikan UEMURA told me to let him move freely during the journey, so I advised him to get out of the cell and act freely, but he kept sitting inside ship's cell, stressing that he was a prisoner. Sir, please bring Mr. Oshima ashore quickly."

Apparently, Daikan could only think of the importance of his own responsibility and couldn't afford to think of SAIGO.

He replied, "I can't decide at my own discretion. Sorry, but please keep waiting on the ship until a prison is prepared."

There was nothing to say any more, and Ryu gave up. He left the Daikan's office and returned to Inobe port.

He told SAIGO about it. SAIGO replied: "I'm sorry to have troubled you. I will feel more comfortable and at ease in the cell."

Ryu, who was responsible for the convoy, could not put up with Daikan's impolite manner, thus he decided to stay with SAIGO on the ship overnight.

2. The Construction of "Windswept Prison"

That night, Daikan TSUDURABARA gathered his assistants and island officials and discussed the construction of prison enclosure. Judging from the contents of the order, it was to be located in a place where it was easier to

watch and they could get a good view of its inside. Thus, they decided to construct it in a narrow place surrounded by the village mayor's office and a sentry box.

The next day, Daikan gathered the carpenters from all over the island. They cut down pine trees from the government-owned forest around Mt. Kosiyama, dug holes at the four corners in a narrow space of less than 8 square meters, and implanted unprocessed logs as props.

Instead of a door and walls, they fastened together thicker logs crossed over each other at equal intervals in a grid pattern. The floor was made of a net of bamboo, tied with thick straw ropes and covered with four sheets of straw-mats. The toilet consisted of two bars bridged over a pit dug in a corner. The roof was covered with thin thatches and the eaves were trimmed short. The toilet was enclosed with screens. There was no furniture except for a brazier.

In this way, a poor, windswept prison was completed in two days.

Around noon on August 16, Daikan finished checking the completed prison and went to Inobe port to meet SAIGO, accompanied by his assistants, Seizo FUKUYAMA and Masateru TSUCHIMOCHI, magiri-yokome (local police officer).

Daikan approached the ship and spoke to SAIGO: "I am Daikan Gensuku TSUDURABARA, As the prison was completed, I came to take you there" SAIGO dressed in a casual kimono made of Satsuma gasuri (a type of cloth made in Satsuma region), put on straw sandals and went out through the narrow entrance of the ship's cell. He stepped down onto the sandy beach saying, "Well, well,

Mr. Daikan, I'm Kichinosuke OSHIMA and will be in your care." He greeted Daikan, FUKUYAMA and Tsuchimochi. He spread his arms and deeply breathed in the ocean air.

Daikan continued, "It is 1 ri (approximately 4Km) away from here to Wadomari, so we have prepared a horse for you. Please ride on the horse." SAIGO refused, saying, "I appreciate your kindness, but I am a criminal. Please let me walk, because this may be my last time to tread on the soil." Then he started to walk slowly with steady steps.

Some of the villagers who had been watching the scene were deeply impressed by his politeness and modest attitude and were moved to tears. Especially, Masateru seemed to have had an intimate feeling for him since then, because there was something about his personality that distinguished him from others.

They all sympathized with him, and followed him silently.

They walked up a slope and came to a tea-house named "Morohakudo", where they took a rest, drinking tea. It was usually used by the officials from Satsuma, who had finished their duties and would return to Satsuma, while waiting for ships.

Even in the afternoon, the summer sun glared down on them, and they kept walking, wiping sweat off their brows.

The top of the slope formed a part of the island ridge, commanding a fine view of the coastline and the boundless Pacific Ocean.

SAIGO stopped walking for a second to look at the distant Pacific through a row of pine trees, and just then the last words of his late lord, Nariakira, crossed his mind:

"Now is not the time for domains to fight with each other. We should look at foreign countries, and cooperate with them to build a strong country. We must not lag behind them." Using a terrestrial globe, the lord told him how remarkably foreign countries had developed.

Now that he could not put into action his lord Nariakira's intentions, he regretted his helplessness. Tears ran down his cheeks.

The road was running downhill. The houses along the road were of a subtropical architectural style. Each house was surrounded by a stonewall and big trees. Around the time when the sky was set ablaze by the sunset, the party arrived at the prison. Daikan said: "We have prepared a little welcome feast. Everybody, please join us." SAIGO said, "I appreciate your courtesy, but a criminal should not be allowed to accept such an offer. Please confine me in the prison right away." RYU and the observer were astonished to see the prison and were at a loss for words. Daikan whispered awkwardly, "I'm sorry to have prepared such a shabby prison, but ....."

SAIGO didn't mind it that much. He said, "Oh, what nice smell the thatches and the natural trees have! I'll be able to enjoy it." Then, stooping his head, he entered the prison through its narrow entrance. Touched by the courtesy and broad mind of SAIGO, Masateru came to feel deeper and deeper respect for him.

SAIGO said to the jailer: "Lock the door tightly so that both of us can feel secure." Then he sat in Zen meditation on the straw mat and closed his eyes. This was the beginning of his harsh prison life.

The reason why SAIGO was exiled to the remote

islands of Tokunoshima and Okierabu-jima and the sequence of events is given below.

In 1858, the Edo Shogunate began to sweep away the royalists in order to protect its duration and stability, which caused a big incident, the Ansei Purge.

SAIGO hid himself in Tatsugo village in Amamioshima during that time, in order to escape from Shogunate officials' pursuers. After that, Shogunate power began to go into decline rapidly. the Tozama daimyo (a nonhereditary feudal lord) came to power. Three years later, he got permission to return to Kagoshima, his domain.

The feudal lord was Tadayoshi SHIMAZU (16 years old), but Hisamitsu, Tadayoshi's father, gained real power under the name of the Father of the Satsuma Domain. Tadayoshi was too young to be a lord. As soon as SAIGO returned to the domain, Hisamitsu gave him the following order: "I intend to go to Kyoto and Edo with 3,000 soldiers and plead with the shogunate to reform its administration. You have connections with each domain, so you must accompany us. You should leave far in advance, gather the information in Shimonoseki, and wait for us there."

As per order, SAIGO, accompanied by MURATA, arrived in Shimonoseki, where they got the information about the situation in Kyoto that was beyond control. It concerned the rumor that the feudal retainers of Satsuma were preparing to attack the shogunate as soon as Hisamitsu would get to Kyoto. SAIGO thought that it was imperative for him to go to Kyoto quickly and dissuade them from doing so, because it was against Hisamitsu's intention. That is why he left a letter to Ichizo OKUBO and

left for Osaka without waiting for Hisamitsu and his attendants to arrive.

Meanwhile, Hisamitsu, who arrived at Shimonoseki three days later, was enraged at SAIGO and his followers, because they ignored his order and went up to Kyoto without permission. He ordered the chief retainer to seize them at once and exile them to some island. Ichizou OKUBO worried about SAIGO and left for Osaka in advance to find out what his real intentions were. They met at the seaside in Hyogo, and talked. Both thought it was difficult to placate Hisamitsu's anger and then began to talk about each other's state of mind.

OKUBO: "Even if you are exiled to an island, it is not clear when you will be able to return. I am responsible for having advised Hisamitsu to take you. Let's die by each other's hand, shall we?"

SAIGO: "Only I should die, but if both die now, what will become of our friends fighting for the emperor? Who will change the history of Japan? Now we had better survive and wait for the time to come. In case the moment does not come at all, we shall take measures accordingly.

By complying with the decision to be exiled to a remote island, SAIGO wanted to prevent the domain from falling into confusion. Besides, he didn't want his friend Ichizo OKUBO to lose the position he had attained. The next day, SAIGO, Shinpachi MURATA and Shinzo MORIYAMA were ordered to return home and stay on board a ship at Yamakawa port in Kagoshima. One and a half months later, SAIGO and Shinpachi MURATA were exiled to Tokunoshima and Kikaijima islands, respectively. Shinzo Moriyama committed suicide during his vogage

there on the ship.

While on Tokunoshima island, SAIGO spent his time reading and mountain climbing. One day, he went mountain climbing, guided by a boy named Nakayu RYU. When on the mountaintop, SAIGO was staring at Amami-oshima island, which lay to the north.

Nakayu: "Sir, what are you looking at? That island is larger than Tokunoshima island, and many people live there."
SAIGO: "Yes, that's right. It has many inhabitants."

SAIGO was thinking of his beloved wife Aikana and children living on Amami-oshima island.

When SAIGO was going down the mountain, he met an old woman who was carrying wood on her back. She spoke to SAIGO.
Woman: "I hear that this is your second exile. I have never heard of anybody exiled for the second time. They say misfortunes never come singly. I hope that you will turn over a new leaf and become a great samurai (warrior).
SAIGO: "Yes, I'll do my best."

SAIGO just listened to what the old woman was saying, head bent. SAIGO felt tense listening to her admonitory but warm words. Later, he learned that her father had been exiled, too.

Two months later, SAIGO's wife Aikana and his two children who lived in the village of Tatsugo on Amami-oshima island came to see him. The parents and their children were reunited after seven months of separation, and SAIGO was overjoyed about this. He embraced two-year-old Kikujiro and three-month-old Kikuko and was

so happy that he became speech less. Tears were streaming down Aikana's face. However, their family's joy was short-lived. An order for another exile was delivered to SAIGO. He read it and seemed to lose all his strength for a moment. Still, he pulled himself together and said, looking at people around: "This time, I am to go into exile on an island that lies farther south. Fortunately, they spare my life."

It was SAIGO's way of mitigating things. People were looking for words to comfort him, but could only put their heads down. Aikana felt sorry for her husband and was sobbing. She was filled with hopeless feelings about the lord's cruel decision .

SAIGO could not believe that what he had talked about with OKUBO at the seaside in Hyogo had become a reality. "In case the right time doesn't come at all, we shall take measures accordingly." The time had come. He had to prepare himself for death.

The following day SAIGO was moved to the village of Inokawa on the same island, while Aikana and the children returned to that of Tatsugo .

The above is the gist of SAIGO's re-exile to Okinoerabujima island. This exile to the island was considered punishment for a felony next to a capital crime. Moreover, the property of the SAIGO family was confiscated, and his younger brothers were put under house arrest.

3. The Rocky Road (Prison Life)

In leap August, 1862 (early October according to the new calendar), despite early fall, the burning sunlight

filled the prison since morning. In a sweat, SAIGO spent his days reading, or sitting with his legs crossed in Zen style and meditating. He was confined in such a narrow space that he could not escape, and his heart was seized with feelings of loneliness through long, long days. Masateru kept patrolling every morning and evening.

Disregarding his duties, he warmly talked to SAIGO about recent events and his studies. Masateru's visits were the only pleasure for him. As for the meals, his attendant, Kuboichi TANAKA, cooked barley rice in the morning for the three meals. Thus, SAIGO ate miso soup with barley rice and some greens for breakfast. For lunch and dinner he poured boiling water into the cold rice and ate it with salt. He obeyed his punishment confinement faithfully, giving up his favorite tobacco and snacks.

As time went by, the toilet started to smell worse and worse, attracting swarms of green bottle flies. During daytime, he was bothered by their buzzing, and in the evening swarms of striped tiger mosquitoes attacked him. He was allowed to take a bath once a month in the bathtub outside the prison. Masateru advised him to take a walk around the prison after taking a bath. However, he refused his suggestion, because such a behavior against the order was imprudent. Thus, after taking a bath he immediately returned to his cell.

Under all circumstances he kept his presence of mind. Even though he made up his mind to die, he sought for enlightenment, and came to the understanding that life and death were one.

Moreover, he continued practicing ascetics in order to realize divine providence.

Though he had done nothing wrong, he had a raw deal. However, this didn't mean that he was not angry with his lord. He wrote two Chinese poems in large characters on the screen and recited them repeatedly every day. By doing this, he suppressed his anger. One of the poems was written by Akashi domain's retainer Shosai MIYAKE in prison:

Not concerned with social status and honor, long life or short life.
Looking straight ahead. I devote my whole soul to spiritual discipline and hold my beliefs firm like a rock.
Haven't I learnt this during these forty years?
Therefore, I can be in prison in peaceful mind with settled beliefs (an iron will).

The other one was a death poem written by Shinzo MORIYAMA. He committed suicide during his voyage on the ship after he was returned toYamakawa with SAIGO and MURATA. It read as follows:

My beloved mother, please do not lament what happened to me. Since ancient times it has been the destiny of all loyal people. Though my death is near, I am just the same as I ever was. I am just going my own way. I blame neither the heavens nor the people.

SAIGO thought that he would make the prison the most suitable place for his self-discipline by having the above two poems before his eyes. When he was young, he studied Zen with OKUBO under Musan, a Buddhist monk of Shoko-ji temple near his house. Taking

advantage of the opportunity of his imprisonment, he decided to continue to practice Zen as a method of self-discipline.

Seeing SAIGO sitting in Zen meditation, Masateru brought him wooden clappers. Masateru said, "It is inconvenient for you, isn't it? Please beat these clappers when you need my help." He was very pleased to receive them, but he never beat them. Masateru asked him, "Why didn't you use them?" He replied, "Because there was no need to use them".

One evening when Masateru called on him at the prison, he had put out the light, and sat in utter darkness. He asked him, "Why don't you light a lamp?" He replied, "Oh, my dear Masateru, I'm ashamed to say that hearing the sound of waves at night reminds me of my children in Oshima and brings tears to my eyes. Human beings are weak, aren't they? They try to discipline their minds, but unconsciously tend to remember their pasts in their minds No, no! I saw you and started complaining. Forgive me !"

As Masateru could find no words of consolation, he said, "You are too good for a man like me." and bowed his head. When Masateru was leaving, SAIGO gave him an anxious and beseeching look.

Typhoon rains with strong winds continued. On one of such days, in the evening, a roaring wind blew through the lattice door into SAIGO'S cell. The sea water, which was flowing backward in a nearby brook, was crashing on coastal rocks and carried by the crosswind. And the splashes reached the prison.

SAIGO tried to protect himself from rain and wind

with a kind of a screen. He spent all night shivering with cold. The next day, Masateru, who was concerned about SAIGO, visited the prison early in the morning.
Masateru: "Sir, you had a terrible evening with heavy rain, didn't you?
SAIGO: "Is it so? Why, the rain is elegant at times, too, I think. Fortunately, I managed to compose a nice poem last night. I myself admire it. Here it is."

He handed a manuscript to Masateru. And then Masateru asked him about its meaning. He replied as follows:
SAIGO: "*The crosswind is beating the torn-off leaves of bananas, while a nightingale is pleading its innocence so loudly that its throat might bleed.*

When I recite a poem of 'Riso' (a poem by 'Kutsugen' –a Chinese scholar and a courtier) on such a night, I feel much more miserable because I have been exiled to the southern island.."

Furthermore, "This is one more poem, another one, too, I wrote earlier." said SAIGO, showing Masateru the slightly wet draft poem in the nearby basket, and then explained its meaning briefly. Its title was 'Gokuchuyukan" (What one feels in prison) and its meaning is as follows:

In the morning, one is treated courteously by one's lord, but in the evening buried alive in a hole.

One's fate is changeable like a cloud in the sky.

Hollyhock flowers are always blooming toward the sun even on cloudy days.

Even if I, too, can neither forge my destiny nor become free, I always intend to continue to keep loyal to my lord in my mind.

All my companions in Kyoto died, and yet it seems strange that

only I am alive and living comfortably on a solitary island in the southern sea.

It is natural that life and death, given to us by heaven, are beyond human power. Even if I have lost my life, I hope to leave only my soul behind in this world and protect the emperor.

(Note) Of 199 Chinese poems composed by SAIGO NANSHUO, the first one was this "Gokuchuyukan". This tells us how deeply he adored the emperor while hovering between life and death. It is noteworthy that of the two heroes, SAIGO NANSHU and Kaishu KATSU, who contributed to the opening of the gates of Edo castle without any bloodshed, KATSU etched SAIGO's said poem into a stone monument and named it the "Ryukon Monument" (that of leaving the soul in this world). The monument is near to his family's burial plot.

Because of bad food and lack of exercise, SAIGO's body was growing weaker and thinner day by day, and his voice lost its strength, too.

Masateru usually ordered his housemaid to deliver to the prison nutritious food cooked by his mother, such as fish, meat, vegetables and the like. However, SAIGO usually expressed his gratitude to her, but never touched the food, so she had to take the food back to Masateru's house. Masateru asked: "Sir, Why don't you eat the food I have my maid deliver?"
SAIGO: "Thank you for your great consideration, but the face of a dead person who has been eating good food is said to be ugly, while that of a person who has been eating coarse food is said to remain beaming."

SAIGO's reply remained incredible to Masateru. Nevertheless, when he saw him smiling faintly, he could not hold back his tears. SAIGO continued to endure the Domain's unjust treatment without complaining. He trained his spirit by practicing Zen meditation, reading books and contemplating. Masateru felt the nobility of SAIGO's soul in his honourable conduct and kind words addressed to him whenever he visited SAIGO during patrol. He said to himself, "I ought to save SAIGO at the sacrifice of my life." He was determined to give his right arm for that, even if he would receive every kind of punishment.

The Instructions of SAIGO Nanshuo
Chapter 25

Deal not with the man, but with Heaven. Be sincere and reflect on your insincerity instead of blaming others for their mistakes.

4. Masateru's Tact- the Soul of "Revere Heaven, Love People"

Now let me talk briefly about the personal history of Masateru TSUCHIMOCHI.

His father, Tsunamasa TSUCHIMOCHI, was a feudal retainer of the Satsuma domain, who was ordered to work for the Okinoerabu-jima magistrate's office and came to the island in 1831. After that, he came to the island three times, and held an important position such as Yokomeyaku (police officer), Tsukiyaku (magistrate's assistant) and

Daikan (magistrate). During the same period, he married Otsuru, who was born and brought up on the island, and had four boys. His first-born Masateru was taken to Kagoshima at the age of four with him when he returned to the domain.

Masateru spent his childhood receiving strict education at the head of TUCHIMOCHI family. He returned to his real mother Otsuru on the island at the age of 14. Masateru, who had returned to the island, worked for Okinoerabu-jima Daikansho, because his academic talents were highly evaluated. And now he had a fateful encounter with SAIGO.

Since then, he was attracted by his sincere personality, and Masateru struggled to save him at the risk of his life.

It was late autumn. A cold North wind came to blow even on the southern Okinoerabu-jima island. In the prison, the offensive smell was getting worse and worse. The wind carried it all around. However strong SAIGO's will might have been, he could not go against the natural course of things as long as he was a human being. His beard covered his face, his reddish hair grew bushy, and his cheekbones protruded. Moreover, his large eyes became indented and lost their brilliance. Though he wore two kimonos one over the other, his dirty body was chilled to the bone. The prison had only one brazier made in Ryukyu, which Masateru had brought there. Whenever a cold wind blew in, SAIGO shrugged his shoulders and held his hands over it. Masateru patrolled the prison every day like a watchdog and couldn't look at his figure without tears. Irrespective of his own duty, the feeling that he wanted to

save SAIGO at any cost grew stronger and stronger. One morning, when he started patrolling the prison, the words written in the order, - Confine in an "enclosure"- came to his mind. He noticed that the room made by dividing the inside of a house (zashikiro) would come under the scope of "enclosure".

About three months had passed since SAIGO was put into the prison. Masateru, who noticed the difference between a windswept prison and an enclosure designated for confinement, thought that it might be a possible way to save SAIGO. Immediately he went to the Daikan assistant, Seizo FUKUYAMA, and talked to him. Fukuyama had regularly heard about SAIGO's condition, and wanted to save him, too. He encouraged Masateru to apply to Daikan. Masateru immediately went to the office of Daikan TUDURABARA.

Masateru was very excited and started to speak, breathing heavily: "Sir, I have a favor to ask of you. It is about Mr. Oshima. He is growing thinner and worn out these days and looks like a ghost. If this continues, he will pass away soon. Please move him to an enclosure prison designated for confinement as written in the order, because this prison he is in now is not an enclosure, but a real prison. I will buy a house, in which I will make an enclosure, so please move him there."

Daikan: "You noticed a good point. I agree with you completely. I will prepare the money to buy a house. I will provide workers at your command to construct the house as soon as possible. The case will be under your care.

Masateru: "Sir, Daikan! I express my deep gratitude for

your decision. I will carry the work out with responsibility.

Masateru was so happy that he almost ran to SAIGO.

Masateru: "Sir, Sir! I got Daikan's permission. You can come out of this prison today."

SAIGO: "Mr. Masateru, what do you mean? I cannot understand what you are talking about."

Masateru calmed himself to explain what had happened.

They both were moved to tears. And then SAIGO stretched out his thin and weak hands through the lattices to hold Masateru's shoulders tightly, while Masateru, too, held out his hands, placed them on the shoulders of SAIGO, and they hugged each other sobbing.

The Instructions of SAIGO Nanshuo
Chapter 24

It is the universe that makes the path of duty for a man. So the man should tread on it, aiming at revering Heaven before anything else

It is very important to love others as much as you love yourself, because Heaven loves you and others equally.

Looking at SAIGO's face drenched with tears, Masateru's heart almost broke with joy, because he felt that SAIGO had had a narrow escape and his life had been saved.

Heaven gave a new road for SAIGO, who had overcome his ordeal.

They say that to devote oneself to others is to place oneself in a state of unselfishness. Masateru threw away his

self-interests, was sincere, and gained the benevolence of Heaven. Though he realized that to live might be more painful than to die, SAIGO was touched to tears by Masateru's un common thoughtfulness and was wiping tears running down his face. He decided to cling to life and follow the path of Heaven with wisdom and courage all his life.

His great motto -"Revere Heaven, Love People"- was born inside the prison and carried out outside into the world.

The jailer came to unlock the entrance door. SAIGO walked along the lattices with unsteady steps. As soon as he got out, he placed his hand on Masateru's shoulder and they went to Masateru's house. The house was 100 meters from the prison and they walked the way shoulder to shoulder. Daikan was so moved by Masateru's adoration for SAIGO that he permitted to construct a new prison. Moreover, he nominated Seizo FUKUYAMA to a surety and his residence to Masateru's house until the prison was completed. SAIGO was treated better concerning his meals and daily life.

Early in November, they began to make a new prison. It was to be located on a clean site inside the official's office.

Masateru bought a comfortable house and made an enclosure prison by partitioning off a corner of the house. It was named "ZASHIKIRO"(room for confinement). The construction cost was covered by "DEMASUMAI" (surplus rice) for Daikan's use. At that time, when Daikan collected the rice tax, he used two measures: One was big, and the other one was small. He used a big one when he

measured the tax rice offered by islanders and, on the other hand, used a small one when he sold it. The surplus rice raised by the balance between the big measure and the small one was called "DEMASUMAI", and it was used for Daikan's miscellaneous requirements.

Masateru told the carpenters to spend three days to complete one day's work beforehand. By prolonging their construction work as long as possible, he hoped SAIGO would recover back to health.

SAIGO, who lived in Masateru's house, ate nutritious meals cooked by Masateru's mother, Otsuru, had enough sleep and took a bath every day like a member of Masateru's family. Thanks to that, he was gaining strength day by day and recovered his health. Tucking up his sleeves, he expressed his gratitude, "I became fat like this. Thanks a lot, Masateru, Mom and Matsu" Both Masateru and his mother enjoyed seeing his joyful look. At night, SAIGO and Masateru enjoyed an evening drink. Sometimes, the assistants, FUKUYAMA and TAKADA, joined, and warmed up the atmosphere. SAIGO sometimes got drunk and would begin to sing a song in a loud voice, saying, "Tonight, my favorite Edo-style (Tokyo-style) song". When it came to his song, Masateru was embarrassed to listen to it, because the Daikan's residence was located less than 200m away from there, so Masateru was afraid that too much amusement would cause SAIGO to be punished.

Masateru: "Sir, Please sing in a more gentle voice. This doesn't become a song."
SAIGO: "Ha! ha! ha! ···· you are afraid of Daikan, aren't

you? This is not the prison. You know, there isn't a law that prohibits singing a song, but if I should get censure, FUKUYAMA, please enter this prison instead of me, because you are my surety."

They looked at one another and then broke into laughter. The atmosphere there became more and more pleasant.

Looking at his refreshed smile, Masateru was filled with a heartwarming feeling.

5. Daily Life in Zashikiro (Room for Confinement)

In about twenty days, the Zashikiro was completed, so SAIGO moved there from Masateru's house. Zashikiro, with a floor space of approximately 7.3m², was made inside a house of approximately 20.7m². It was well ventilated, well lit, and its underfloor was high. Furthermore, it had not only a bathroom, but also a separate toilet, so it was very sanitary.

SAIGO: "Masateru, thanks to your help, I got a good retreat. It is luxurious for an exile." "By the way, please bring the charcoal brazier made of paulownia wood from the warehouse." SAIGO said to Masateru.

Masateru: "You have such a good brazier, though. Why didn't you use it?"
SAIGO: "Ah, Ha, Ha, ···· Masateru, in the previous prison, the brasier you had given me was enough, but this time I would like one suitable for the new house which is like a palace. This was my important treasure bestowed by late

lord Nariakira."

The house with the zashikiro had walls, doors and was spacious. A man named Kuboichi was to take care of SAIGO. He came to the zashikiro every day, opened and closed the doors and prepared meals. SAIGO was allowed to take a bath every other day instead of once a week and to take a walk as well. He got some freedom. As for meals, Kuboichi prepared meals typical for a prison. Besides, SAIGO was glad to have some side dishes delivered from Masateru's house.

After SAIGO moved to the zashikiro, his living conditions improved, but he never slipped into self-complacency. He neither offended against the order, nor escaped from his fate. While staring at the moon shining in the night sky, the memories of the previous prison came to his mind. It seemed strange to him that he was still alive when he remembered several days he had spent in such a delirious state, when he could not distinguish between day and night". Heedless of his duty, Masateru made a direct appeal to Daikan to save me while I had been struggling with adversity. "I will love others just as I love myself." This was the way of Heaven, earth and nature (Heaven's will)". SAIGO, who was illuminated by the moonlight, expressed his gratitude for Masateru and his mother, placing his palms together.

And now, SAIGO, who had been reborn, made up his mind to live a long life, to dedicate his life to Masateru, his mother, the islanders and people in general.

6. SAIGO-Juku (Private School) and His Disciples

SAIGO spent most of his everyday life in the zashikiro, reading. He was so absorbed in reading, to the extent of making reading a "part of his body". When Masateru saw him sitting upright and reading, his respect for him grew deeper and deeper. Once Masteru said to him, "Sir, please teach your knowledge to local children. They seem to want to learn to read books." SAIGO was glad to do it and asked Masateru to gather the children.

Several 15- or 16-year-old boys, including Tankei MISAO, were willing to join SAIGO-juku and become his pupils. Remembering the former Goju (education for the samurai in Satsuma Province), SAIGO used both individual instruction and group lecturing. His manner of teaching was very polite and proved to be very effective.

Basically they had a reading lesson in the morning and a lecture in the evening. However, SAIGO juku's teaching style was very unusual. SAIGO was lecturing from inside the enclosure, while his pupils sat straight in the corridor outside it, only to listen to him. SAIGO's education at his juku was nothing but an expression of his enthusiasm. That is to say, he hoped that giving education to the disadvantaged young people of an isolated and remote rural area will turn them into full-fledged adults.

The main books taught at SAIGO-juku were:

★ the Four Books and Five Classics of Confucianism,
★Kinshiroku (a book of Chinese thought)
★Genshiroku (self-improvement and philosophy book by

Issai SATO)
*Omeikaniso (Collection of literary heritage of Heishu HOSOI)

Most of them were related to human life, morality, politics and studies. SAIGO's pupils put the great teacher's teachings into practice, and gave a good example to others by taking the initiatives and carrying them out.

Those young people served as waiters for several days at Daikan's or officials' residences or offices. It was "on-the-job training" to learn good manners to become officials. They were called apprentice officials.

SAIGO-juku made a lot to train the pupils as apprentice officials, making them acquire practical knowledge such as greetings, polite wording, manners, etc. Those were the first steps toward becoming officials.

In the New Year, new apprentices entered SAIGO-juku, totalling around 20 students.

SAIGO sent the following letter to the SHIIHARA brothers, his uncles:

I spend my time reading books, and my students totalled around 20. I enjoy prosperity and as it is said that in the country of the blind, the one-eye man is a king, I read to my apprentices from morning until noon and lecture them at night.

Strange to say, I feel like a scholar. However, my prison life enables me to persue my studies."

Though SAIGO-juku lasted for only a little more than one year, its influence was so great that the endeavour for learning was kept by his disciples, the second- and the

third-generation of students after he returned to the domain. SAIGO-juku formed the basis for the development of Okinoerabu-jima island..

One morning when a boy named Tankei MISAO came to clean the prison, SAIGO said to him, "Tankei, you seem to like learning very much. What do you think you should do in order to make a family live in harmony?" From the phrases he had learned, Tankei replied instantly, "It is to live up to the five human relations (father and son, lord and vassal, husband and wife, old and young, one and one's friend) and the five eternal virtues of Confucianism (humanity, justice, courtesy, wisdom, sincerity)". "HaHaHa! you memorized it well, didn't you?", said SAIGO. That was a good opportunity to teach him practical studies, he thought. SAIGO wrote something and handed the paper to Tankei, giving explanations.

"It is important to live up to 'the five human relations' and 'the five eternal virtues', but if you adhere to the words, you are a person who only gets things half finished. The best way is not to be greedy. It is very important for the whole family to be so sincere as to share tasty food and have clothes made according to the order of ages from oldest to youngest.

A word of "greediness" worsens warm relations between parents and children or between relatives. Therefore, if you remove your greediness, which is often the cause of discord, their affection for you will last forever."

In Okinoerabu-jima island, there were more than 30 private schools, including SAIGO-juku. Some of them were run by other exiles, and ohers by the islander

scholars. The island enjoyed a better learning environment than any other island. The island, full of enterprising people, produced officials, doctors, teachers, lawyers and other professionals.

In Meiji era, the school system was established, and, at the same time, a study session at each community, including Akataji student institute, Wadomari kosinsha and others took the place of the previous juku. The entire community supported the education of young people.

The exiles of Okinoerabu-jima island were regarded as felons, who were different from common criminals, but most of them were scholars or political criminals, who were eminent in both learning and virtue. It goes without saying that the foundation for the development of education, culture, politics, economy, life, etc. on Okinoerabu-jima was built by such exiles as SAIGO and others.

7. The Coming of the New Year

The new year of 1863-the year of the boar of the Chinese Zodiac- came to Okinoerabu-jima island. SAIGO was born in the year of the boar and became 37 years old. Moreover, he was born in a year with the same sign of the Chinese zodiac as the current year.

1 kin (600g) or 2 kin of pork was delivered to the prison to celebrate the new year. Masateru and his mother visited the prison with hearty food and drinks. They raised a toast, sitting on different sides of the partition, inside and outside of the enclosure.

That year in March, Daikan TSUDURABARA and his

assistants finished their two-year-term of office and were supposed to return to Kagoshima. FUKUYAMA and TAKADA were old friends and were sad to part.

TAKADA gave his short sword to Fukuyama and asked him to give it to SAIGO in case he had troubles without wearing a sword when he returned to Kagoshima. Later SAIGO sent a thank-you letter and a grateful poem to Takada.

(outgoing predecessor) (1861〜1862)

Daikan	Gensuke TSUDURABARA
Assistant	Seizo FUKUYAMA
	Jinzaemon MIKIHARA
Police Officer	Heijiro TAKADA
	Shichinosuke YAMAGUCHI

(Incoming successor) (1863〜1864)

Daikan	Heizo YAMADA
Assistant	Genzaemon KITO
	Manjiro KAWAGUCHI
	Gensuke AKAZAKI
Police Officer	Hachinojyo KAMADA

The new Daikan YAMADA visited the prison to meet SAIGO to report his arrival. After exchanging courteous words, they had the following exchange:

Yamada: "Mr. Nakayama told me to give his best regards to you and look after you carefully."

SAIGO: "You are Daikan, aren't you? Daikan must not tell a lie. Mr. Nakayama could not have asked you to take care of me."

SAIGO answered back angrily, while Yamada tried to convey the message to him with his utmost effort.

Masateru, who was nearby and heard their conversation, was worried that it might cause trouble to SAIGO. Indeed SAGO had been exiled because of the slanderous words of Shonosuke NAKAYAMA and some other people. Therefore, Daikan Nakayama's message sounded false to him. Later, however, Nakayama noticed that SAIGO had been right and that he himself had been wrong. That's why he had made an effort to pardon him. SAIGO had no way of knowing that fact.

8. SAIGO and Seppo KAWAGUCHI

Seppo KAWAGUCHI(initially Kazujiro), who was called Koun as a calligrapher, lived in Nishibaru village as an exile. It was about ten years since he had been exiled to this island in 1851. His ancestors came from Tanegashima island, but he was born and brought up in Edo. When young, he mastered Yomei-gaku (the teachings of Wang Yang-Ming). He was an expert in calligraphy and was well versed in poetry, too. He lived in Kagoshima as a copyist for Hisamitsu (lord of Satsuma Domain), but was exiled to this island by “renzasei” (a system of collective responsibility) because he was considered responsible for his father's and brother's misconduct. In Nishibaru village, he opened a private school and produced many disciples. Among them were Ichigen HIGASHI, NISHIMURA, KASHIWA, IKEDA and others, who worked as doctors or teachers.

Then Seppo was 46 years old, SAIGO's senior by 9 years. Soon after SAIGO returned to the domain, he was returned to Kagoshima, too, and lived with his son-in-law

for a short period of time. Then he stayed as SAIGO family's guest and got a teaching job at a private school. After SAIGO's death in battle, he supported SAIGO's family and died of disease at the age of 73 in 1890. The inscriptions on Takamori SAIGO's and Shinpachi Murata's tombstones in Joko-ji Temple in Kagoshima city had Seppo's calligraphy.

Seppo called on SAIGO at his prison under Masateru's permission. He had been attracted by SAIGO's personality, the warmth of his heart, humility and sincerity since they met for the first time, while SAIGO was charmed by Seppo's bright and easygoing personality or by the fact that he did not hanker after wealth and fame. That's why SAIGO had a close relationship with Seppo.

Seppo liked to drink and often visited the prison with a bottle of sake. While drinking, he often discussed history, the prosperity of the nation and initiated into calligraphy and poetry. They talked, forgetting time.

"I envy you, a prisoner, because you can eat without working." Seppo joked and laughed away. He would often be tired from talking and would fall asleep, snoring in the corridor of the prison.

"The word of 'a sleeping teacher' is the perfect one to describe you." SAIGO pulled his leg. Seppo responded. "Oh! 'A drunken sleeping teacher' is OK." Their chats never ceased.

One early morning when Seppo left Nishibaru, he got lost on the way. While he was taking a rest in the field, a grass-cutter passed by. He showed Seppo the way, and he managed to reach the prison safely in the evening. SAIGO heard him come, and said, "I've never heard that someone

was deceived by a fox in the daytime. I am sure you were absent-minded. From now on, I will call you 'a stupid teacher' instead of 'a sleeping teacher'." "Have it your way. As for the name, the more names one has, the better." They engaged in animated conversation and rolled with laughter.

At present, judging from SAIGO's calligraphy, there is no doubt that it was influenced by Seppo's style of calligraphy. Most of SAIGO's poems were composed after he left Okinoerabu-jima island. He started writing poems in earnest after learning poetry under Seppo.

Chapter 2

Reborn SAIGO

1. Reborn, Regarding Heaven as His Mentor

The New Year in 1863 had just passed, and the season when the warmth of early spring was felt came. The stream close to the prison rose after a long period of rainy days. Many frogs at the bank were croaking loudly.

Masateru said to SAIGO, "The islanders are busy with farm work: planting sweet potatoes, plowing the plots of sugar canes or wheat. They are busy working till late at night every day."

After hearing Masateru talk about agriculture, SAIGO remembered that when a little boy, his father took him to their radish field, and he helped him with spadework. His father said to him then, "You are the eldest. You can't take care of your younger brother and sister with a lower–ranking samurai's (warrior's) salary alone, so you have to continue working as a farmer." He intended to follow his father's advice. However, after he began attending on his brilliant and honest domain lord, Nariakira, he had to spend most of his time in Kyoto and Edo doing the domain's work. His lord treated SAIGO as his right hand and taught him how to do the job. He explained to him the state of affairs in foreign countries, and showed him which way Japan should proceed.

SAIGO was told the following story by his ally, Sanai

HASHIMOTO: Nariakira told Echizen's lord, Shungaku MATSUDAIRA, that it was only SAIGO that he could rely on in an emergency among many retainers, and that only he could use SAIGO, who had an independent spirit, successfully. From this, we can learn how strong the bonds between the lord and his retainer were. SAIGO seemed to regret that when he had learned about the death of Nariakira, he could not follow him to the grave. Nariakira was not only a master to SAIGO, but a life mentor.

When SAIGO was exiled to Okinoerabu-jima island, with Masateru's help, he narrowly escaped death in prison. After that, he looked up to Heaven as a mentor during the latter half of his life. He decided to cling to life and live as long as possible. He was reborn, regarding "Revere Heaven, Love People" as his supreme motto.

Kuboichi, his man-in-waiting, opened the door to the corridor before he knew it. The morning sun poured into the prison, and a balmy spring breeze was blowing.

His cell, called zashikiro (room for confinement), was far more comfortable than his former one. Though it seemed narrow, SAIGO stretched his body, breathed deeply, and exercised his arms and legs. He ate the food with delight, which Masateru's mother, Otsuru, delivered to his prison. As a result, it seemed to Masateru that SAIGO had gained weight and recovered strength. Above all, Masateru was glad that SAIGO became cheerful and spiritually positive.

He was an ordinary person, who performed storytelling, talked with Seppo and those who visited the prison, and excited the islanders with his favorite sumo, while he was

a prisoner, with distinct individuality, too.

2. "A Prison Teacher" Plays Sumo

SAIGO's living environment was improved after he moved to Zashikiro (room for confinement), and his treatment concerning food and body exercise became better, too. He enjoyed communication with the islanders. He became emotionally stable and was recovering his original strength.

"Masateru, thanks to you, I've gotten better. I don't know how to express my gratitude to you, but I want you to see my energetic self through sumo wrestling, so please look for an opponent in sumo for me."

As Masateru had heard before that SAIGO played sumo, he was glad to search a sumo opponent. He brought the strongest wrestler on the island, Bokujyun MATSUO. Immediately, a make-shift ring was made in an open space (sand beach) in front of the prison. Of three matches they had, the one who won two was declared the winner. Both got slightly nervous, surrounded by many spectators. SAIGO, who was adept in sumo, won two in a row, and was declared the winner. He was showered with grand applause from spectators. This news spread all over the island on that day where there was no information network, and his name was widely known as 'Mr. SAIGO, the Sumo-Wrestler'. Local people called him 'Prison Teacher' and treated as a close friend, with much intimacy. SAIGO came to be widely respected by rustic pure islanders and given the honorific title "Prison Teacher".

SAIGO said to Masateru, "Are there any other sumo

wrestlers?" Three days later, Masateru brought Sangoro, who was a rice boiler for Daikan's assistant, Manjiro KAWAGUCHI. He had not only a gigantic and muscular body, but also a lot of experience. He was proud that he had been unbeatable in sumo wrestling. "Well," said Sangoro with self-confidence before the match began: "A big difference between powers may cause serious injury." The match venue was crowded with so many spectators that a fence was set up. The match started. "Come on, Prison Teacher!" A great cheer went up from the crowd. Both fought to the best of their skills and bumped against one another. SAIGO, who was superior to Sangoro in technique, threw him in the center of the ring. SAIGO won two matches and was declared the winner. "Prison Teacher" became a hero of the island.

Masateru was glad that SAIGO had regained his strength. Moreover, feeling that he was taught how important it was "to do with sincerity", Masateru wept with joy.

3. Storytelling and a Fan

These days SAIGO seemed to feel grateful for his peaceful life even in prison. Masateru patrolled every day, Kito came to the prison to talk about the world situation, and Seppo's teachings of poetry and calligraphy were fun, too. He was called "Sir! Sir!", and respected by his 20 students from the bottom of their hearts.

Besides, interesting messages were sent by both Manjiro KAWAGUCHI, an official in charge of Yoron-island, and Sukeuemon MERA in Okinawa. He felt happier and happier to realize that nothing was more valuable than human

compassion.

On one of such days, after finishing his job, Masateru visited the prison with food and drink. He was looking forward to seeing SAIGO's smile and hearing his story. After a few drinks, SAIGO felt pleasantly tipsy and said as usual, "Today I'll tell you a military story. Give me a fan." He borrowed the fan Masateru had brought and turned over a tobacco-tray. Beating it with the fan, he talked comically about 'Musashi MIYAMOTO' or 'Soga brothers'.

Masateru finished listening to his tales and then made fun of him, saying "Sir! Your tales are enjoyable, indeed. They are first-class ones, but the fan is broken to pieces, so it is now useless. Five or six fans have already been damaged so far. I want you to make up for them." He responded with a smile, "My military story cost me much. You have listened to them for free without paying money and, on top of it, it's a bit too much to expect me to pay for broken fans." Both burst into laughter.

4. Gago (Pseudonym) - "Nanshu"

Around early fall in 1863, the village mayor Teiryo SO delivered eggplants to the prison. They were excellent in color, smell and taste. They were Masateru's mother Otsuru's home-made ones. Moreover, a Japanese poem attached to them was most delightful. In return, he wrote the following Chinese poem as a token of his gratitude:

Thanks to you, I am very happy to be able to relish the eggplants with quite rare, beautiful, glossy color and the same delicious taste

as before. I have to appreciate your deeply compassion. Your lovely poem attached to the amazing eggplants was the greatest pleasure and delight.
Respectfully, Nanshu

★For the first time SAIGO used his pseudonym "Nanshu" in this poem. It means "a southern island" and he made it his pseudonym.

5. Teaching Political Foundations

SAIGO was convinced that Masateru, who had saved his life, would take a position like Yohito (high ranked official) to carry the future of this island on his shoulders, and put the instructions for Yohito into shape. Then SAIGO gave them to him as "Yohitoyaku-daitai" (instructions for high ranked officials) and "Yokomeyaku-daitai" (instructions for police officers). The contents were so realistic and concrete that incumbent officials appear to continue putting them into practice.
The key points were as follows:

(1) Yohitoyaku-Daitai (Acquaintanceship of Officials)

1 Officials are in the most important position that protects islanders' lives and property. If one of them did anything wrong, he would lead thousands of or tens of thousands of people in the wrong direction. Therefore, they have to take even trivial matters into careful consideration and carry them out cautiously.
2 The most important thing is to gain people's trust. As

soon as they think that they can control people at will, they will lose people's trust and make enemies of all.
3 Really good officials always think of not only people's worries and troubles as their own, but also their delight and pleasure as their own, and conduct politics in accordance with its foundation- The God's will.
4 It is very important for farmers to contribute to the nation through their labors.
They need to increase production and accomplish both liability to taxation and imposition of labor completely.
5 If even Daikan's order worries farmers, good officials try to explain to him that the order is difficult to carry out and remonstrate him. If it is reasonable, their trial is not lese-majesty, but official's important fidelity. Therefore, it goes without saying that it is important for them to bear this in mind.

(2) Yokomeyaku-Daitai (instructions for police officers)

1. The first role of police officers is to produce no criminals. It is nothing but a trifling matter that they are good at finding, arresting, or examining them.

2. It is important to sympathize with such disadvantaged people as widows, widowers, the aged, children etc. help those who suffer from hardships and mental agony, and motivate people to help each other .

3. It is their important role to treat criminals fairly, based on the law so as not to punish criminals with minor offences heavily and vice versa, and make them understand their punishments.

Masateru was appointed to Yohitoyaku (village mayor) after SAIGO returned to the domain.

Needless to say, he took both Yohitoyaku- and Yokomeyaku-Daitai for his model. He spent much time looking around the villages to advise and encourage the farmers, with whom he shared joys and sorrows without self-interest. He was nicknamed "Tsunachino-shu (master of Tsuchimochi's Family)" and respected by them. His nickname was sung in a friendly, rustic ditty:

Ohitotsu meshiagare, Tsunachino-shu (Have a drink, please, Tsunachino-shu)
Mohitotsu mesiagare, Tsunachino-shu (Take one more, please, Tsunachino-shu
Sai (rice wine), Sai, Sai, Sai muchiku, nudiashiba
(Bring Sai, Sai, Sai, and let's enjoy drinking)

For more than 30 years Masateru was in a leading position such as Yohito or Kocho(head of a town or a village), and contributed greatly to the development of the island.

He should be admired as the very first man that practiced SAIGO's idea of "Revere Heaven, Love People"

<Nanshuo Ikun 4> (a collection of lessons by SAIGO)

Those who direct people must always control their minds, conduct themselves properly, and admonish themselves against luxury and haughtiness. Besides, they must devote themselves to their duties efficiently and serve as people's model. Only when they work so hard that everybody feels sympathy for their jobs and lives, they can execute their political orders well among people.

In spite of the beginning of the Restoration, however, if administrators think nothing but decorate their houses, wear luxurious clothes, keep their concubines, and save their properties, they are not able to fully achieve the true results of the Restoration.

Now the Boshin War fought for justice caused them to pursue their personal greed. That's why, SAIGO felt remorse for the nation and the war dead, and shed tears frequently.

6. Teaching Famine-Relief

In the early autumn of 1863, SAIGO wrote two instruction books - "Yohito-yaku Daitai" (instructions for officials) and 'Yokome-yaku Daitai' (instructions for police officers)-, which he gave to Masateru.

He was not sent to the island under a mission of governing the island and its people. He had been sent to the island as a criminal. He paid more interest than Daikan and other officials in that he wanted the islanders to have better and more purposeful lives.

Okinoerabu-jima island surrounded by the sea was visited by typhoons every autumn. They caused serious salt damages and spoiled farmers' yearly harvest in a day. In the summer, droughts damaged crops seriously, too.

It depended only on rain and dew whether the harvest would be rich or poor, because the coral island had low-lying land and no mountain that could provide water supply. It was historically recorded that great famines caused by natural disasters such as typhoons, droughts, etc. had ravaged the island many times.

One day when Masateru visited Zashikiro (room for confinement) as usual, SAIGO welcomed him, smiling unusually.
SAIGO: "Masateru, Okinoerabu-jima island seems to have various kinds of natural disasters like typhoons or droughts. Assuming that these cause severe famines and that lots of people starve to death, how can you help people as an official ranked above islanders?"
Masateru: "This island, as you know, is a small, isolated one, so there is no better choice but to beg Kagoshima's lord to help.
SAIGO: "Indeed Okinoerabu-jima island is a small, isolated island just as you say. The lord will send relief supplies on your request. However, it may happen that typhoons and seasonal winds will prevent ships from sailing for several days. It will take you quite a number of days only to go to Kagoshima for begging. If it takes so many days when islanders are on the brink of life and death, all of them will starve to death. How do you cope with these circumstances as an official, being responsible for protecting islanders' lives and properties?"
Masateru was at a loss what to answer, and all he could do was to hang his head down. Looking at Masateru, SAIGO said: "In such an emergency, the most important thing is that all the islanders work together to get over their ordeal. Nothing in this world is stronger than united efforts. It ends in failure 'to depend on the power of others' or 'to put yourself under others' wings'.
In old times, during the period of Sung Dynasty in China, residents in each area made shaso storages with united hearts, which enabled them to get over their great

famines over years. As all the islanders in Okinoerabu-jima need to unite and face famines together, I'll show you how to make a shaso storage." Then he wrote a "prospectus for Shaso storage", and gave it to Masateru.

(1) A Prospectus for Shaso Storage (extract)

To provide against a bad harvest or a famine, it is quite important to gather and store crops through frugality in an abundant year. As for the collection method for storing crops, it is necessary to examine each farmer's surplus of rice, millet and wheat, take the number of family members into consideration, and allot the amount of contribution to each family fairly. Farmers will accept this very comfortably. Naturally, the importance of benevolence based upon the spirit of 'Shaso storage' will be achieved.

For example, if the stored rice reaches 5 koku (approximately 750Kg) in total and is rented at a rate of 20% per year, it will produce one koku (approximately 150Kg) interest a year later. As the years go by, the stored rice will increase remarkably in amount. Therefore, it is possible that the five-koku rice initially stored will be returned to the farmers who had contributed surplus rice. After that, only interest rice will be invested.

In this way, that is to say, by saving those who have had a mishap or feeling pity for the disabled people, it will become possible to help unhappy people. In case of famines, the Shaso storage' will be appreciated as a gift from Heaven by those in great difficulty, and their hardships of long standing will be repaid. After all, it is important to provide against a year of famine beforehand in order not

to get flustered in an emergency. Originally, farmers offer service through their labor, while officials do through their intellect and spirit. It is quite important for both farmers and officials to do their best to serve.

7. Building of Hoon-maru Ship
"The Namamugi Incident" and "Anglo-Satsuma War"

Hisamitsu SHIMAZU went to Edo as an escort of an Imperial envoy, Shigetomi OHARA, who would convey the Imperial order concerning the reformation of shogunate administration to the Tokugawa shogunate, and made the Shogunate accept Yoshinobu as a guardian of young shogun Iemochi Tokugawa and Yoshinaga MATSUDAIRA as the president of political affairs, respectively.

After carrying out his mission, on his way back to Kyoto, he came across four English merchants riding on horses, including Richardson, when he reached Namamugi village (Today's Tsurumi ward of Yokohama city) on the afternoon of August 21, 1862. Then one of their horses ran into the feudal lord's procession, which caused confusion. Kizaemon NARAHARA, the head of the procession, drew a sword, slayed Richardson and injured two other men for their rudeness. This was the outline of the Namamugi Incident.

England was angry about the Namamugi Incident and demanded that the shogunate government should apologize and pay the amount of 100,000 pounds as compensation, and that Satsuma domain should extradite the criminal and pay the surviving family 25,000 pounds in consolation money. The shogunate accepted its demand, but Satsuma domain refused to comply. After that, England and Satsuma domain negotiated several times, only to fail. England's charge of d'affaires judged that they had no choice but to

appeal arms. On June, 27 of the next year, 1863, he sent a British navy fleet consisting of HMS Euryalus and six war ships to Kinko Bay in Satsuma. They continued to negotiate for two days on June, 28 and 29, but both didn't yield an inch. As a result, on the morning of July, 2, the battle started. It was the so-called Anglo-Satsuma War.

Around the end of autumn in 1863, SAIGO finished writing a 'prospectus of Shaso storage' and gave it to Masateru. After that, he lived a peaceful prison life. Suddenly, however, he received the news that the Anglo-Satsuma War had broken out in Kagoshima.

The information was considerably exaggerated. It ran as follows: England's navy consisting of dozens of warships entered Kagoshima Bay, and the castle town was almost burned down. Satsuma's ships were sunk one after another. A lot of people were killed in the war. The shogunate supported England. There was no advantageous information for Satsuma at all.

SAIGO was unable to restrain himself. In particular, he was shocked that the shogunate had tied up with England and attacked Satsuma. All he could do in his anguish of mind was to give a deep sigh.

Masateru called on SAIGO at his prison as usual. "Sir! Is there anything you are concerned about? Please let me know."

SAIGO: "Masateru! You have come just at the right moment.

In fact, I hear that a war broke out in Kagoshima. England's navy opened fire, and the town was burned down. Many people appear to have been killed and

injured. I am worried about that. I'm thinking that even if I repeat offenses, I'll go up to Kagoshima immediately. I want to be useful for the people no matter what."

Masateru: "Is the war breaking out in Kagoshima? My father lives there, too. Please take me with you, because I'm worried about him."

SAIGO wanted a ship to escape from the island, but he could not find one. He dared to consult with Masateru.

Listening to his hard-pushed story, Masateru promised, "I will construct that ship." He confessed it to his mother Otsuru.

She responded, "You are wonderful, my son. I will help you make the money to construct a ship. A ship constructed by a woman is said to bring good luck." Masateru and his mother cried with joy.

She told her two servants, who had lived together like real family members, to come and then talked about not only the war in Kagoshima, but also shipbuilding expenses for SAIGO to rescue his country from crisis. Then with tears in her eyes she begged them to change masters to make money. They agreed, saying, "It is more unbearable for us to leave your warm family than death. Please let us change masters to help SAIGO and all of you. We'll keep your favors in mind throughout our lives and hand them down to our posterity."

Thus, both servants left Masateru's family for their new masters in Yakomo village and Minagawa, respectively, so they could have a possibility to make money.

SAIGO was very glad. His family had some servants, too, but he didn't think that he could do what Masateru and his mother Otsuru had done.

He composed a poem about Tsuchimochi family's heroic deed and sincere loyalty, and gave it to Masateru.

To Masateru TSUCHIMOCHI

Your sincerity is in no way inferior to the noble spirits of the past. You are filled with high spirits to repay the favor of your master whole-heartedly. It shows your true feelings that you pay attention to world affairs widely and devote yourself to shipbuilding. The way you had sold your servants with heart-breaking grief and broken off a relation between master and servant to raise funds is quite uncommon. I want you to follow your mother's teachings and throughout your life serve not less faithfully than your ancestors. I hope that you will devote yourself to national affairs without bias and without favor, and that you will outdo excellent persons with pure and great ambitions.

SAIGO made an application for a transfer of government forest in order to get big trees for constructing a ship, and submitted it to Daikan in the name of Masateru. According to the application, his main purpose was to construct a ship:

(1) to apply for reinforcements to Kagoshima when foreign countries invade the island

(2) to escape from the island when an upheaval happens in Kagoshima

"The application for a transfer of timbers for a ship" was approved immediately, so they started logging the forest and constructing a ship. The ship was completed in early November and was named HOONMARU.

Meanwhile, a merchant ship on the Ryukyu line happened to put in at the port with an information of the ending of the Anglo-Satsuma war. SAIGO inquired of

Sukeuemon MERA in Okinawa about more details by letter. His letter revealed the following:

"On the morning of July, 2, the steamship, Tenyumaru and the other two, which had been concealed in the sea area off Shigetomi, were captured and burned down.

The captains, Tomoatsu GODAI and Munenori TERASHIMA, freed their subordinates and became their prisoners voluntarily. They were taken to Yokohama together with England's navy fleet. Then the domain gave orders to open war, and every battery set on fire all at once.

One of England's warships at anchor near Yokoyama Battery in Sakurajima cut off its anchor chain and ran away. It was taken by surprise, and had no time to heave up its anchor.

Our shells burst on the bridge of the flagship, HMS Euryalus, and the captain, vice-captain and some others were killed instantly. The battle continued on the 2nd and 3rd days when a typhoon blew violently. On July 4, the navy fleet left.

In this battle, ten people died, eleven were wounded, and five hundred houses were burned down. Furthermore, some batteries and Shuseikan were destroyed. Three steamhips and some Japanese-style ships were lost." (After that, Satsuma paid war reparations, and established friendly relations with England. It sent 19 students to England to study. - monument : a group of Satsuma's young men)

It was about two months later, in early October, that SAIGO, confined in a room, got reliable information. Hoon-maru ship, built after great pains didn't need to be used for achieving its original aims, but Tansai MISAO, the village mayor, was determined to use it to go up to

Kagoshima as a messenger in order to express sympathy after the Anglo-Satsuma War.

Besides, as Tansai wanted to beg the domain's government to arm Okinoearabu-jima island with guns, he asked SAIGO to write a petition. SAIGO took a pen, wrote the petition in a very polite language and handed it to Tansai.

Its summary was as follows:

1. When enemies invade, and we cannot defend ourselves successfully, we are worried that Okinoerabu-jima island is not only stigmatized by foreign countries, but also in danger.

2. We see no other way but to ask you to arm the remote island of Okinoerabu-jima with guns. We want about ten guns of 10 mon caliber (1 mon≒2.4 cm) immediately.
3. If it is impossible, we want at least one. We pay for them with sugar next spring.

November,28,1863

Soon Tansai MISAO went to Kagoshima. SAIGO gave him two Japanese poems as a wish for a successful journey.

For the lord, the ship navigates the open sea
The god of wind, don't blow and ruffle the surface of the sea
Oh, God! Keep the ship filled with the islanders' sincerity safe, when going and returning

8. A Pledge of Brotherhood

More than one year passed since SAIGO's exile to the island. SAIGO never forgot Masateru's warm and heartfelt friendship. "If it had not been for Masateru, I might have already passed away and become earth on this island", he thought. So, whenever he saw Masateru, his heart was filled with "gratitude" and "nostalgia". At such moments, SAIGO was eages for him and Masateru to become sworn brothers. The more often they met, the more they talked, the stronger their relationship became. SAIGO wrote a letter to Masateru without hesitation. It said, "Tonight, as I ask a favor of you, please come to me with your mother. Please, take sake and snacks with you." It was the first time for SAIGO to ask for sake and snacks voluntarily, so Masateru was very glad. His mother Otsuru was very glad, too, and did her best to prepare a feast. Then both visited the prison.
SAIGO: "Mom, I'm sorry to bother you. Masateru is my important savior. When I was on the verge of death, he saved my life. It was a narrow escape. I am alive, and I totally owe that to Masateru.
Otsuru: "Even though he is always near you, I'm sorry he is full of shortcomings.
A paper-framed lamp with two blazing wicks was illuminating the faces of the three men separated by the lattice. They began the "exchange of sake cups", each of them offering and being offered a sake cup.
Soon SAIGO sat up straight and spoke to Otsuru.
SAIGO: "Actually, Mom, I have a special favor to ask

both of you. That is why I asked you to come here tonight. Masateru is my savior. He was very kind to me and took scrupulous care of me. I do not think he is a stranger. Mom, please I beg you to allow us to become brothers."
Otsuru: "How nice of you to think so about Masateru! Does he really deserve it? My heart is full of gratitude. I am grateful. Sir! Please make Masateru your younger brother."
Masateru: "Sir! This is really too good for me. Thanks a lot for your care."
SAIGO: "Thank you for your permission. Well, Mom, please give me a cup of sake."

Otsuru handed a sake cup to SAIGO in the enclosure. Her heart was filled with joy, and her hand was trembling a little with too much joy.

Returning the cup to Otsuru, he said, "Please, from now on think of me, too, as your own child."
SAIGO: Saying, "Masateru, though I am a trivial man, I'll be your elder brother, because I'm older than you." he gave another cup of sake to Masateru.
Masateru: "Sir! No! Bro, I've never been so happy in my life."

SAIGO "Well, then, Mom, we exchanged cups of sake as a pledge of parents and brothers. Now Masateru and I became sworn brothers. Let me sing a song I learned in Oshima."

I have neither parents nor relatives in this island. Persons who love me are my parents and relatives.

Otsuru: "I will sing a song of tonight's joy, too."

Though we are strangers, we wonder how friendly we are. We wonder how our hearts are fitting in. Or, is it an old relationship?

Masateru: I will sing, too.

May a relation between us last until a young pine tree grows old.

Their delight reached climax. SAIGO stood up, took out an inkstone and paper and wrote a poem fluently and easily. He said, "This is not a complete Chinese poem, but it is the expression of my heart. I'll give it to you to keep in mind our meeting tonight" and handed it to Masateru.

Then SAIGO and Masateru were 37 and 28 years old, respectively.

Of the things we usually see, there are many unfavorite ones, but I found that the heart-to-heart interaction with you was quite different from ordinary affection. I dislike those who covet words and behave immorally as if they were my enemies. I would like to share my fate with those who control their selfish desires and are extremely sincere. I trust you from the bottom of my heart, and you, too. I am younger than you, and I call you my elder brother. You are older than me, and you call me your elder brother. Talking of our deep friendship so far, it will help us devote ourselves wholeheartedly to our people and to our country.

In May 1863, conflicts between kobu-gattai (integration of the imperial court and the shogunate) party and sonno-joi (reverence for the emperor and the expulsion of foreigners) party became serious.

Choshu domain, in which the latter party had a strong power, tried to expel foreigners from Japan by force by attacking American merchant ships, Dutch and French warships crossing the Shimonoseki straits with gunfire.

On the other hand, America and France protested against the shogunate and attacked Shimonoseki as a reprisal. It was seriously damaged. As Emperor Komei preferred the idea of Kobugattai to that of Sonno-joi, he was studying countermeasures to cope with the situation together with the following members of Kobu-gattai party:

Katamori MATSUDAIRA (Aizu domain),
Yoshinaga MATSUDAIRA (Echizen domain)
Hisamitsu SHIMAZU (Satsuma domain)
Toshimichi OKUBO (Satsuma domain)

As a result, seven court nobles, including Sanetomi SANJO, who belonged to Sonno-joi party and Choshu domain, which had guarded the Imperial court, were swept away and escaped to Choshu. This was the so-called "Coup of August, 18".

Thus, the movement of Kobu Gattai centering on Satsuma and Aizu, lasted for a while.

Choshu, which had been forced to leave Kyoto, called Satsuma and Aizu "Satsuzoku Aikan" (retaliation against the Satsuma and Aizu Domains), and the relation between Satsuma and Choshu was getting worse.

After that, in Satsuma, the conflict between Kobugattai party and Sonno joi was getting more serious. Therefore, everybody keenly felt that a new leader was to appear.

<Nanshuo Ikun 20> (a collection of lessons by SAIGO)

Whatever system or method may be discussed, things don't go well unless its persuader is excellent. An excellent person comes first and a method comes second. That is to say, a person is the most important treasure. Nothing is more important than to endeavor to become such an excellent person.

9. " Movement to Pardon SAIGO " Breaks Out

Satsuma, which had been attacked in the Anglo-Satsuma war, began to feel hostile towards the shogunate, centering on the Seichu-gumi Organization (a volunteer group of middle and lower ranked feudal retainers). That is to say, the Shogunate forced Satsuma to take responsibility for the Namamugi Incident, which had caused the Anglo-Satsuma War, because it trembled with fear of a protest from England. Satsuma took this as a serious problem that would affect the fate of not only the domain, but also the country and concluded that SAIGO was the only person to cope with the situation and overcome the crisis.

Seichu-gumi and the comrades, who were implicated in the Teradaya Incident, agreed and started a movement to plead with the lord to pardon SAIGO. (Teradaya Incident: Hisamitsu ordered to attack and purge the members of Seichu-gumi Squad of his own domain, who belonged to sonjo party (royalists) and gathered in Teradaya inn in Fushimi in Kyoto.)

However, Hisamitsu had such a deep-rooted hatred for SAIGO that he could not get rid of it so easily.

In January 1864, the 13 feudal retainers of Satsuma Domain, including Masakaze TAKASAKI, who had been

stationed in Kyoto, got together and decided to suggest to Hisamitsu that he pardon SAIGO. If their opinion was not accepted, they agreed to immediately commit hara-kiri suicide in front of their lord.

TAKASAKI met Hisamitsu to explain about the world's situation, while he pleaded with him to pardon and call SAIGO back. Hisamitsu listened to him, smoking a silver pipe, but did not reply. Nor did he look back with a pipe in his mouth. He looked quite pale. TAKASAKI flinched, but went on persuading bravely. Hisamistu still kept silent, but Takasaki continued to prostrate himself without leaving. Then, for the first time, Hisamitsu took the pipe out of his mouth and said, "According to you, everybody says SAIGO is a wise man. If so, only Hisamitsu is stupid enough to reject your wish, which does everybody no good. Ask for lord Tadayoshi's decision." In the end, Hisamitsu gave in to TAKASAKI. They say a deep trace of tooth shape was left on the pipe mouthpiece. It was because Hisamitsu was extremely angry and stuck his pipe to find that SAIGO would be summoned. All the feudal retainers of the Satsuma Domain were in Seventh Heaven with joy. Three persons, Tomomi YOSHII, Tsugumichi SAIGO and Seizo FUKUYAMA, were appointed messengers to call SAIGO back. It was the end of January 1864.

10. "Kochomaru" to Okinoerabu-jima to Pick Up SAIGO

After the Anglo-Satsuma war, which had broken out in July, 1863, came to an end, the movement to pardon SAIGO grew rapidly.

A letter from his uncle, Gonbe SHIIHARA informed SAIGO that he might be released and would be able to return to the domain. He bubbled over with joy in his heart, but never lost his self-control. When he was exiled to the distant island of Okinoerabu-jima, he thought that he was as good as dead, and prepared for death. However, he took everything as the will of the Heavens. He overcame all the hardships and engaged in severe ascetic practices. The Heavens continued to let SAIGO live on the island and wait for the time to come.

It was on February 21, 1864 that the steamboat "Kochomaru" with three delegates for releasing SAIGO on board, including Tomomi YOSHII, arrived on the island. About that time, smallpox spread in Kagoshima, so officials on each island quarantined passengers when the boats from Kagoshima arrived and took preventive measures in order not to let ashore the suspected ones.

On that day an express boat arrived at Inobe port, so Masateru was running his horse to the port to quarantine the crewmen. On the way, he came across a running sailor, who was carrying a letter. He asked him about it. The letter appeared to be a pardon for SAIGO. The sailor took the occasion to talk about a boat to pick SAIGO up.

Masateru took out a writing implement and wrote, "Sir, a boat is likely to come to pick you up today. I will hurry to the prison after I finish quarantine procedures." Then he asked the sailor to deliver his letter to SAIGO and ran his horse to Inobe.

While quarantining, a sign of a boat sailing from Tokunoshima to Okinoerabu-jima came into sight, puffing out black smoke. It was the very steamboat, Kochomaru.

Masateru finished quarantine procedures in a hurry and rushed back to Wadomari at full speed. He was impatient to report about the quarantine and visited the prison. SAIGO had already changed into formal dress. "Sir, the boat to pick you up will arrive at the port soon, so get out of the prison quickly, please." He rushed SAIGO. SAIGO said, "Thank you very much for your letter. Daikan Yamada came and read the letter of pardon to me."

Nevertheless, SAIGO was reluctant to leave the prison, so Masateru led him by his hand. Then they climbed up a nearby rock and looked at the sea. The boat was doubling Cape Kunigami, heading for them. That time, SAIGO began fidgeting. They returned to the prison immediately and set about packing. Kuboichi helped them.

Masateru: "Sir! What are you looking for?"

SAIGO: "I think I'll give you a worn-out striped-crepe lined garnment as my keepsake, which I got from my former lord, Nariakira. I have been looking for it, but I can't find it. I wonder where I have put it."

Masateru: "Sir! What is that under your arm?

SAIGO: "Ha! ha! ha!, Look here! It cannot be found as it is under my arm!"

However calm SAIGO seemed to be, Masateru could see on this occasion that he was nervous. SAIGO gave the lined clothes to Masateru.

Flying the rising sun flag and the domain flag with an emblem of a cross inside a circle and making a big splash, Kochomaru was running toward Nagahama beach across the sea in a straight line. Many people gathered on the shore. They were speaking loudly staring in the direction of the boat.

SAIGO and Masateru were moved so deeply that they were speech less. Their eyes were full of tears.

Heaven told SAIGO, who had made a fresh start on the isolated island in the southern sea, that the time had arrived, and entrusted him with an important duty.

It was around one o'clock in the afternoon that Kochomaru dropped its anchor.

A boat with three men in it, including Tsugumichi, left the mother ship and was approaching Nagahama beach, floating up and sinking among the waves.

Tsugumichi jumped down on the beach before a wooden ladder was set up, and made a mad dash for his brother, Kichinosuke, who was in the crowd.

Tsugumichi: "Bro !"

SAIGO: "Oh! You came, didn't you?"

SAIGO grasped his young brother's hand tightly with his big hands. His voice betrayed him. Both shed tears with their heads down. Bending slightly forward, people around there, who were going to meet them, were heard sobbing.

After a while, SAIGO wiped away his tears and looked at YOSHII:

SAIGO: "Oh! Dirty fellow, You came, too!"

YOSHII: "Don't be foolish! You know I am the chief delegate to meet you, What do you mean by 'Dirty fellow' ?"

SAIGO looked at Masateru, and said, "This guy has been a dirty, mischievous boy since childhood, and his nickname was 'lice Goro'.

Everybody burst into laughter. A friendly atmosphere was born. After exchanging usual greetings, SAIGO spoke to YOSHII.

SAIGO: "Shinpachi MURATA, who was exiled to Kikaijima, will return with us, too, won't he?"
YOSHII: "Only you, this time."
SAIGO: "No! It cannot be true that only I will be able to return. MURATA's crime was much lighter than mine.
He must be permitted to return earlier than me. Yes! I will take him with us. Bring round the ship to Kikaijima, and I will take responsibility for that." He insisted. He was thinking more about his friend than about himself.

YOSHII and two other men understood his feelings well and agreed that MURATA would return together with them.

The three delegates were supposed to stay at Okinoerabujima for about a week to observe the conditions on the island, and if possible, the living conditions of the people. However, they decided to return on the next day, because they were running out of coal fuel. SAIGO bade farewell to the islanders and gave his keepsakes to the people who had taken care of him. He gave clothes and a brazier made out of paulownia wood to Masateru and his mother, which he had received from his former lord Nariakira and used in the prison.

He gave most of his belongings he had brought from Kagoshima to the islanders as a token of his gratitude or as keepsakes.

That night a farewell party was held in the office of the village mayor. Daikan YAMADA, officials and local officials participated, and the three delegates from Kagoshima were invited, too. Participants' feelings were a mixture of joy and grief. Some rejoiced about the summons, and oth-

ers were reluctant to part. It was a lively party.

SAIGO took out a piece of paper from his inside pocket, and wrote a farewell Chinese poem. He gave it to Masateru. It ran as follows:

A farewell is empty and restless like a dream or cloud. I am to leave, but I will come back. Tears are flowing incessantly. I do not know how to express my thanks for lots of favors I had received during my prison life. Even after I return to Kagoshima, I will remember you though you are far across the sea.

The atmosphere of the farewell party was also the sadness of parting. SAIGO, Tsugumichi and FUKUYAMA left the party hall, urged by YOSHII. Many people were waiting for them at Nagahama beach to see them off. There many torches were burning brightly. SAIGO and his friends climbed the wooden ladder to board the barge, and then a great cheer went up from the crowd, "Good bye, Sir! Take care!" Among them, there was a person who was screaming, "Sir! Sir! ……Take care of yourself!"

Shouting, "Oh! Shimatomi! ……‥You came, didn't you? "Thank you" ……‥"Thank you" I owe a lot to you. I have nothing with me but this……Keep it as my keepsake…‥ as a token of my gratitude to you." SAIGO took off his vest, tied it with his belt and threw it to the sand beach,

On that day Shimatomi NAGATA finished his farm work earlier than usual and returned to his home in the village of Kunigami. There he received the information from the village office and immediately rushed to the beach. Shimatomi was employed as a cook together with

Kuboichi, and he was waiting on SAIGO.

The barge took SAIGO and the other three delegates to its mother ship 'Kocho maru'.It was around one o'clock in the morning on the following day, Feb. 22, that Kocho-maru weighed its anchor and left for Tatsugo.

Chapter 3

The Dawn of Modern Japan (Meiji Restoration)

1. The Wind Blows From the South

Around noon of Feb. 23, 1864, the ship reached Tatsugo, and SAIGO spent three days and four nights there pleasantly with his beloved wife Aikana and their two children. They were reunited. A year and a half had passed since they had been separated in Tokunoshima.

As soon as Kikujiro saw his father, Kichinosuke, he ran into his large arms. Urged by her mother, Kikuko got on his lap shyly and from time to time looked up to stroke his beard with her tiny hands. SAIGO was holding his two children tightly with a smile, trying not to let them go. Looking at the scene, Aikana was trying to hold back her tears.

In the evening, a large number of villagers came to Aikana's house. They held a lively party. YOSHI and Tsugumichi also took part.

By the irony of fate, in later years, when Kikujiro and Kikuko were 9 and 11 years old, respectively, they were taken over by SAIGO's family in Kagoshima. Aikana, who had been left alone, passed away at the age of 66, worrying about the children's future throughout her life. Her fate was unavoidable, because she married SAIGO, knowing the unwritten rule: "Even if they marry, women are never allowed to leave the island.'.

After leaving Tatsugo, Kocho-maru stopped at Kikaijima Island to pick up his comrade Shinpachi MURATA and then headed straight for Kagoshima.

While on board the ship, SAIGO remembered nostalgically his life on Tokunoshima and Okinoerabu-jima islands.

On Tokunoshima , an old woman gave him words of blessing: "I have never heard before of someone being exiled twice to a remote island. Sir SAIGO, this was your second exile, wasn't it? As the old saying has it, 'Misfortunes never come alone.' You must amend your conduct this time and become a good samurai (warrior)."

On Okinoerabu-jima, when I was about to die in the prison, Masateru TUCHIMOCHI saved me at the risk of his life. He appreciated the warm hearts of the people who lived on isolated islands in the southern sea. Influenced by the islanders who cherished encounters, he himself was awakened by the thought, "Revere Heaven, Love People" and felt a certain joy at being reborn and able to return home. His dream flew to the land of Japan, carried by the south wind.

Mt. Sakurajima which he saw for the first time in a while, welcomed him, shooting volcanic smoke high into the sky. It also gave him courage.

As soon as he reached Kagoshima, he visited his late lord, Nariakira's grave to report his homecoming and vowed to repay him for his kindness. He was appointed Gunbu-yaku (army commander) and a negotiator with various domains by the domain's lord, Tadayoshi. He had no time to take rest and went to Kyoto.

2. The Kinmon Incident and Takamori SAIGO

In the middle of March,1864, SAIGO arrived in Kyoto and met with Hisamitsu and a friend of his childhood, Toshimitsu OKUBO, to hear about the situation in the domain and about the Guard of the Imperial court.

According to what they told SAIGO, the conflict regarding the Imperial court between "Sonno-joi" party (reverence for the emperor and expulsion of foreigners) and "Kobu-GATTAI" party (integration of the Imperial court and the shogunate) was getting more and more violent. In particular, the movement of Choshu, which belonged to "Sonno joi" party, was getting more and more radical. The seven nobles of the Imperial court on the side of Choshu domain were ordered to leave the court. As a result, Choshu domain frequently had skirmishes here and there with the domains on the side of the shogunate, including Aizu, Satsuma, Echizen, Kuwana and some others.

In July, Choshu soldiers who had been driven out from the Guard of the Imperial court bravely attacked three gates, aiming at breaking into the Imperial court again. They tried to destroy Kinmon (Hamaguri-gomon Gate), which Aizu domain had guarded, and break through Rakuchu (inside the court). However, the Satsuma army, which had guarded Inui Gate, hurried to Kinmon to repel them under the initiative of SAIGO and fought bravely to the end.

SAIGO took Choshu's prisoners to the Satsuma domain residence and treated them politely. He gave them clothes

and food. After that, he sent them back to Choshu. In Kyoto city, a fire caused by this battle continued for two days, and around 40,000 private houses burned down. A stray bullet shot his leg, so he was slightly wounded. In spite of his wound, he commanded his army bravely. His fame "There exists SAIGO in Satsuma"–spread all over the country. The battle was called 'Kinmon Incident (or Hamaguri-gomon Gate Incident).

In the incident, the shogunate-side domains won. SAIGO got an opportunity to talk about Choshu Conquest and Kobu-Gattai (integration of the Imperial court and the Shogunate) with the government's naval magistrate, Kaishu KATSU, and his disciple Ryoma SAKAMOTO.

KATSU said, "In the present Shogunate, it is not clear at all where authority and responsibility lie. Now is the time for major domains to combine their forces to move the nation." In spite of the fact that he occupied an important position in the Shogunate, he criticized it. SAIGO was attracted by his width of mind and his personality. In August that year, taking advantage of the momentum in the Kinmon Incident, the Shogunate decided to attack Choshu more intensively.

It appointed Yoshikatsu TOKUGAWA as commander and SAIGO the general staff. He knew what KATSU had in his mind, so he was trying to find a way to win without fighting with powerful Choshu. To do so, Choshu was required to apologize for raising the hand against the Imperial court (Kinmon Incident), and deal with chief retainers involved in the Kinmon Incident on its own responsibility.

Therefore, he visited Choshu and made an effort to persuade them with sincerity. Choshu appreciated the importance of the fact that SAIGO, the enemy's general staff, had come alone and shared his view that the domestic battle was vain. Thus, Choshu domain accepted his argument, and the Shogunate won without fighting. That was the First conquest of Choshu.

In Choshu, to make matters worse, the squadrons from America, France, Holland, and England took reprisals and Shimonoseki was completely destroyed.

(Choshu Domain attacked the foreign ships of the United States, France, etc. that were passing the Shimonoseki Straits to indicate the intention to expel foreigners before the Kinmon Incident)

3. Restoration of Imperial Rule

Taking advantage of its victories in the Kinmon Incident and the First conquest of Choshu, the Shogunate had the illusion that if it just gave orders to Choshu Domain, it would obey them. Therefore, the Shogunate planned and ordered the Second Choshu conquest with confidence.

On the other hand, Choshu Domain reflected on their consecutive defeats in war and integrated its opinion from 'Sonno-joi' to 'Overthrowing the Shogunate'. In particular, Ryoma SAKAMOTO's mediation led the Satsuma-Choshu Alliance. Thus, a military cooperation was established. Thus, Satsuma left the group of the Shogunate.

In June 1866, the Shogunate planned and then carried out the Second Choshu conquest. It was done without Imperial sanction. Satsuma did not participate in the

conquest.

Choshu, which had excellent morale and strategy, prepared new types of weapons to counterattack and won series of victories everywhere.

The Shogunate army was forced into hard battles, while the Shogun Iemochi TOKUGAWA died of disease at Osaka Castle.

Yoshinobu TOKUGAWA, the Shogun's guardian, aimed at recovering authority and encouraged his retainers to rise again. However, they could not withstand the attack of the army of Choshu.

At last, the Shogunate switched its strategy to cease-fire under the pretext of the Shogun's death, and assigned Kaishu KATSU to negotiate, who had been confining himself to his home. Choshu army agreed that the Shogunate army withdrew and Choshu army would not pursue them. The Shogunate's crushing defeat in the Choshu conquest resulted in encouraging the anti-Shogunate groups across the country, which gained more and more strength day by day.

Tosa Domain, from which Ryoma SAKAMOTO came, presumed that the Shogunate would come to an end soon, and submitted a petition to the Shogunate to transfer power to the emperor.

Shogun Yoshinobu TOKUGAWA accepted the petition sincerely, and on October 14, 1867, proposed that it should transfer power to the emperor. On the next day October 15th, the Imperial court issued an edict to approve the memorial to the Throne.

As a result, the Edo Shogunate established by Ieyasu TOKUGAWA in 1603 ended its 264 year-old history. The

restoration of the Imperial Rule led Japan from the long-time feudal society centering on warriors, toward the modern state, advocating 'freedom' and 'equality of all people'. The national politics changed from Tokugawa Shogunate to the emperor.

The footsteps of Meiji Restoration echoed throughout the country loudly and sonorously.

[Background of Restoration of Imperial Rule]

PERRY, an admiral of the East India fleet, came to Uraga port in 1853. According to his request, the Shogunate concluded the Treaty of Amity and Commerce, followed by the Treaty of Peace and Amity. Thus, Japan opened two ports, Shimoda and Hakodate, and offered water and food to foreign vessels. In addition, it opened five ports, including Niigata and Yokohama, and propelled free trade. Woolen textiles, weapons etc. were imported, while silk and tea were exported. However, the customs duties were put into the hands of the countries concerned. The laws of their own countries judged the foreigners who committed crimes. The application of these unequal treaties raised Japan's prices rapidly, which resulted in threatening common peoples' lives. Satsuma and Choshu, which had felt dissatisfied with such Shogunate's policy, started overthrowing the Shogunate in alliance with each other. The Shogun Yoshinobu TOKUGAWA was afraid of public outrage, and transferred political power to the Imperial court. It was Taiseihokan (Restoration of Imperial Rule). However, the former Shogunate armies of various domains in the regions of Tohoku and Hokuriku, resisted violently and fought with the Imperial army, though it

meant fighting against the Emperor. It happened 15 years after PERRY came to Japan.

Instructions of SAIGO Nanshu
Chapter 17

It is impossible to establish diplomatic relations with foreign countries unless you tread on the right path and have a strong spirit to shoulder your responsibilities even if you put your nation at stake. If you fear powerful foreign counties, shrink yourself, and submit to foreign countries against the true motive of your country only to cool down things smoothly, you will be despised and will lose amity. In the end, your country will be conquered by foreign countries.

4. The Boshin Civil War and Takamori SAIGO

After the 'Transfer of Power Back to the Emperor' the Imperial court decided through the Imperial Council upon three offices -President, Legislature, Councilor - to be the nucleus of the new government, and announced 'the Decree for the Restoration of Imperial Rule'. Furthermore, it summoned the leaders of Owari, Fukui, Hiroshima, Tosa, and Satsuma with Tomomi IWAKURA (court noble) as their leader, to open a meeting at the Imperial Palace, and discussed Tokugawa Shogunate's necessity to return all government posts and territories.

Yoshinobu TOKUGAWA listened to the report about the decision at Osaka castle, and was furious that he had been neglected. He launched an attack on Satsuma and Choshu. On January 2, 1868, Yoshinobu proceeded toward Kyoto at the head of a large force of 15,000 soldiers.

The opposing Satsuma and Choshu forces poured gunfire into the former Shogunate forces at Tobaguchi in Kyoto. The fighting began at Fushimiguchi, too, and triggered the Boshin War. The Emperor had already sided with Satsuma and Choshu. Therefore, the former Shogunate forces were regarded as the Emperor's enemy, and surrendered under the 'the Imperial Standard flag'.

Moreover, each domain sided with the former Shogunate forces switched to the side of the Imperial forces one after another. The Commander-in-Chief of the former Tokugawa Shogunate, Yoshinobu TOKUGAWA, tried to escape to Edo, leaving Shogunate retainers to continue fighting. Thus, in the Battle of Toba-Fushimi, the high morale of the Imperial forces and SAIGO's excellent military strategy led them to victory.

In February, 1868, SAIGO was appointed Chief of staff officers of the Imperial army, and headed toward Edo. Yoshinobu, who had run away to Edo, appointed Kaishu KATSU commander-in-chief of the former Shogunate army, gave him the authority to treat the end of the war and swore allegiance to the emperor at Kanei-ji Temple at Ueno. By avoiding a meaningless fighting, KATSU wanted to have a meeting with SAIGO to protect the lives and property of the people of Edo, and make him guarantee tens of thousands of the former Shogunate retainers' lives. Tenshoin (wife of Iesada), and Kazunomiya (wife of Iemochi), who had married into the Tokugawa Shogunate family, submitted a petition to the Governor-General to save the life of Yoshinobu, and maintain the continuance of the Tokugawa Family.

KATSU met SAIGO twice upon Katsu's request. The

two great men were congenial spirits and the meeting had a friendly atmosphere. An all-out attack on Edo Castle on March 15, was stopped, and the city escaped war disaster. In April, 'the bloodless surrender of Edo Castle' was transferred to the Imperial army officially. After the meeting with KATSU, SAIGO reported the results to the governor-general, and went to Kyoto to hold the meeting between the three offices with various reports. SAIGO made extraordinary efforts and managed to achieve a great success over a short period of three weeks.

5. The Shonai Domain and Takamori SAIGO

Edo Castle, Tokugawa's headquarters, was bloodlessly transferred to the Imperial Palace thanks to the decision achieved during the meeting of the two great men, SAIGO and KATSU. However, several domains of Hokuriku and Tohoku regions, which were under obligation to Tokugawa, still continued to resist, hoping for Tokugawa's comeback. It was absolutely necessary for the Imperial Court to construct a unified country to propel Japan's modernization. The Imperial army centering on Satsuma and Choshu was forced to fight back and forth fiercely with great sacrifices. SAIGO's younger brother Kichijiro SAIGO said: "This time I want to be helpful, too", and offered his participation in the Echigo-Nagaoka war.

Unfortunately, he died in the disadvantageous battle. SAIGO was able to take part in affairs of state so far, thanks to Kichijiro, who had devoted himself to household affairs. He always felt deep respect towards Kichijiro. He was grieved to learn about Kichijiro's death with his

hair cropped short.

Each domain in Tohoku and Hokuriku fell one after another. Only Shonai domain was powerful enough to fight fiercely. However, it used up all its strength, and surrendered to the Imperial army.

The ceremony regarding 'surrender' was held at the auditorium of a domain school named Chidokan (Confucian school). All the armed retainers waited inside anxiously.

Kiyotaka KURODA, a general staff of the Satsuma domain, entered the auditorium with several soldiers. KURODA took the seat of honor and read the Instrument of Surrender to Tadazumi SAKAI (16 years old), lord of Shonai Domain, who took the less important seat. Then KURODA delivered the conditions of surrender. It read, "The lord should take a rest at the family temple, and follow the great path of the Restoration of Imperial Rule. All the retainers should put a rein on their own behavior, and be allowed to carry a sword as a warrior status." On finishing reading, KURODA took Tadazumi, the domain lord, by the hand, and led him to the seat of honor. And then KURODA took a less important seat himself, and, putting both his hands on the floor, said, "I have just officiated as a messenger, but from now on I treat you with the utmost courtesy as the Domain Lord." The retainers were prepared to take strict revenge. They were deeply moved by KURODA's generous treatment. It was because it was Shonai Domain that had set fire to Satsuma residence in Edo a year before. Knowing that KURODA's every action was based on SAIGO's order, people of Shonai Domain felt gratitude and respect towards SAIGO's virtuous behavior.

They admired SAIGO's virtue and more than 100 people, including Tadazumi SAKAI, domain lord, Sanehide SUGE, chief retainer, from 1870 till 1876 visited Kagoshima all the way to learn SAIGO's teachings. Later, in 1889, the domain retainers compiled the teaching in a book entitled "Nanshuo Ikun" (a collection of teachings of Takamori SAIGO). It was done based upon Suge's order.

In the following year, Shonai Domain's retainers traveled across the country to distribute the books.

6. The SAIGO Cabinet and SAIGO's Humble Private Life

In the Boshin War that started from Toba-Fushimi battle and continued through Edo, Tohoku-Hokuriku, and Hakodate, after bitter battles, Imperial forces gained the final victory. It seemed strange that Satsuma and Choshu, which were in a minority, could ally themselves and get over their difficulties. It can be said that SAIGO's disinterested sincerity, magnanimity, and courage, that is, his credo-"Revere Heaven, Love People"- helped them to win.

After then, SAIGO refused to serve the Meiji Government, and returned to his hometown, Kagoshima, where he enjoyed taking walks in the woods with his dog and having hot-spring treatment.

In 1869, in the granting of honors, SAIGO was rewarded 2,000 koku (rice: 1koku≒144kg) as the highest Shotenroku (additional rice stipends) by the new government. He was appointed to Shosanmi (Senior Third Rank). However, it was higher than feudal lord's rank, so he refused to accept

it, because he did not think he deserved it. In that year, the Meiji government carried out Hanseki Hokan (return of lands and people to the Emperor).

It was the greatest problem for the Meiji government to abolish domains, positions of domain lords and domain retainers. Thus, the government resorted to the practice of Haihanchiken (the abolition of domains and establishment of prefectures). It laid the foundation for building a modern nation where all people would be free and equal. It was unavoidable for all the feudal lords and retainers across the country to resist Haihanchiken. Therefore, it was apparent that the Meiji government would be confronted with major difficulties. Thus, the government applied for SAIGO's help repeatedly. However, he continued to refuse. At last, the Meiji Emperor sent his envoy to SAIGO, which made SAIGO decide to go to Tokyo. In other words, the Meiji government had no choice but to depend on his popularity and ability.

In June 1871, as the head Councilor, SAIGO summoned influential people to carry out Haihanchiken. After that, amid the sweeping tide of modernization, SAIGO established such enterprises as post offices, banks, and railways. Furthermore, he reformed such systems as compulsory education, land tax, police, conscription etc. Remarkably, he appointed Tetsutaro YAMAOKA and Tomomi YOSHII as the Emperor's educator, and took measures to bring up a physically and spiritually strong Emperor.

In November of the same year, a party of 48 members, including Toshimichi OKUBO, led by Tomomi IWAKURA was sent to Europe and America. Their formal purpose was to negotiate for treaty revision to break

off unequal treaty concluded during the Shogunate period, and study things Western. That is to say, during the unstable period just after the serious issue-'the abolition of domains and establishment of prefectures-lots of influential members of the new government were sent abroad, while SAIGO and so on remained, and administered affairs of the state.

What was SAIGO's private life like? His monthly income as a Councillor amounted to 500 yen (equivalent to 1,500 thousand yen at today's prices). Even though such an income should have enabled him to live such a luxurious life in a mansion like other high officials, he rented the former Himeji Domain's warehouse-residence at Koami-town, Nihonbashi, at three yen per month. It had only two rooms, a drawing room and a room for KUMAKICHI and other employees. His monthly living expenses were about 20 yen, which seemed to suffice. As for the remaining amount, young people, including students from Kagoshima, brought back as much money as they needed. Furthermore, the final remaining amount was contributed to Zoshikan (a domain school for samurai children). He walked to his office, had rice balls wrapped in bamboo sheath or buckwheat for lunch, and wore a single kimono made of Satsuma kasuri (a type of cloth made in the Satsuma region). Actually, regardless of his appearance, his simple and plain private life continued for three years. His popularity was due to his modest and plain lifestyle, too.

7. The Subjugation of Korea and the Seinan War

In May 1873, a misunderstanding of the official documents sent to Korea caused a diplomatic problem between Japan and Korea, which caused such a threatening move as prohibition of import of Japanese products, deportation of Japanese residents, etc.

The new government tried to continue negotiations with Korea, but in vain. In such a situation, an insistence on the subjugation of Korea (supporting military pressure to force Korea to open the contry) rose in the new government. Thus, a cabinet meeting was held, and decided to send SAIGO to Korea as an ambassador. The grand minister of state, Sanetomi SANJO, extended SAIGO's dispatch to Korea, because he was going to get an Imperial sanction after the IWAKURA Mission to Europe and America returned home. In October, the IWAKURA Mission returned home, and the Cabinet meeting was held again to dispatch SAIGO to Korea. As a result, SAIGO's dispatch to Korea was decided again. However, as SANJO suffered from a high fever and fell unconscious, IWAKURA came to take up the deputy of the Grand Minister position and report SAIGO's dispatch to Korea. When IWAKURA reported the Cabinet's decision to the Emperor, he reported his private opinion inspired by OKUBO and others, too, (It's desirable to suspend to dispatch SAIGO to Korea)

As a result, SAIGO's dispatch to Korea was postponed indefinitely. At that time, SAIGO made a decision to resign from all the positions, and renounce his ranks. IWAKURA persuaded him to remain in his positions, but

SAIGO resigned lightheartedly. Followed by him, Councilors Taneomi SOEJIMA, Taisuke ITAGAKI, and Shinpei ETO resigned. Remarkably, over 600 people, including high-ranking government officials and Imperial Guard officials, who admired SAIGO, left the government. SAIGO's title of an army general remained as it was, which was the measure to prevent soldiers' turmoil.

SAIGO called on OKUBO at his house to say farewell the day before he left for Kagoshima.

OKUBO neither answered properly nor saw him off. That was the last conversation exchanged between the two, who had worked for the nation for a long time together since the time they were boys.

This issue on Takamori SAIGO's dispatch to Korea was the trigger for Seinan War in later years.

After SAIGO returned to Kagoshima, he established a school for little boys, and a private school with the Shotenroku (additional rice stipends) as his contribution to the Restoration. The government officials, who had returned home together with SAIGO, played a central role in school management. Children whose parents had died in the Meiji Restoration were preferentially enrolled in these schools. The number of students continued to increase year-by-year, totaling up to as many as 30,000 in both the principal school and branch schools around 1876. Furthermore, SAIGO established Yoshino Reclamation Company in the Terayama plateau, where students had a passion for building a utopia to develop their spirit of self-reliance and independence through farming at daytime and learning in the evening, living on rice mixed with sweet potato. SAIGO lived under the same roof with his

students, carried a manure wooden pail on his shoulder, and tilled with a hoe.

After SAIGO and others left the government in October 1873, a new government centered on IWAKURA and OKUBO was born soon. To begin with, the new government reformed the land-tax system, and then introduced new systems one after another. In 1874, rebellions against the government rose in various regions. The rebels in Saga, Fukuoka, Kumamoto, Yamaguchi, etc. raised their fervor, which continued to torment the government. The government was worried about the movement of SAIGO or his private school.

On February 1, 1877, SAIGO happened to go hunting with his dog in Konejime in the middle of Osumi Peninsula.

"God damn it!" Looking at the face of his younger brother, Kobe SAIGO, who, uttering a grievous cry, brought him the news, SAIGO slapped his thigh hard.

"The private school students found that the government army was carrying out the ammunition from the powder magazine in Somuta to the ship, so they are trying to take it back. That's why the whole town is now in confusion." Kobe reported in a trembling voice. SAIGO kept silent and occasionally looked at Kobe with his big eyes.

Store houses, where weapons and ammunition were kept, were located in three places in Kagoshima: Somuta, Iso, and Uenohara. Each store house was managed by the prefectual office. The government army tried to carry out the ammunition without getting in touch with the prefectural office in advance and did it secretly at night. That caused the government army and the private school stu-

dents to scramble for it.

The government made spy's slip into Kagoshima, plotted SAIGO's assassination, and was irritated by the private school's movement since long ago. The government, which felt critical, planned to deliver the ammunition and weapons to Osaka early, and that led to the incident.

It was two days later that SAIGO returned to Kagoshima from Konejime.

After he listened to the detailed account of the incident, SAIGO determined that there was no choice but to question the government about his assassination and the spy, and said to his close aides, "I'll devote my life to you all." Everything was settled. Thus, they raised their fervor, and decided to go to Tokyo. At first, they thought that they would organize their troops inviting the private school students to join. They numbered 1,300.

However, not only former samurai warriors in Kagoshima Prefecture, but also those from various regions in Kyushu who respected and admired SAIGO joined the troops. As a result, the troops numbered 30,000 immediately. It was noticeable that Sotaro MASUDA, who had referred to SAIGO's personality-'If you come in contact with Mr. SAIGO for one day, it will beget love for one day, and if you do for three days, love for three days will be born.'-organized Nakatsu-tai troops and joined them.

On February 17, 1877, Kagoshima had a heavy snow fall for the first time in 50 years. Army General SAIGO in informal dress was proceeding east through Iso Highway.

The government army appointed Lieutenant General, Aritomo YAMAGATA, and Vice Admiral, Sumiyoshi

KAWAMURA, to general staffs to subjugate the SAIGO army, and set up the governor-general headquarters in Osaka.

The government knew that the SAIGO army had left Kagoshima, and sent reinforcements to Kumamoto. At 1 o'clock at night on February 21, the spearhead of the SAIGO army led by Shinsuke BEPPU was assaulted by the government army at a place 8 kilometers away from Kumamoto.

The SAIGO army noticed that, and went on the counteroffensive against the government army, and made it retreat. That was the start of the Seinan War. When he left Kagoshima, SAIGO ordered his troops,"Never fire from us." That is why it was clear that the government troops challenged the SAIGO army to a fight. This offensive and defensive battle at Kumamoto-jo Castle were fierce, and many soldiers on either side died. The SAIGO troops greatly troubled the government ones, which outnumbered them in every sector – in arms, weapons and ammunition by the Drawn Sword Squad. However, The SAIGO troops were attacked from behind by the government ones, which had landed at Yatsushiro, and they lost many brave soldiers, including Battalion Commander, Kunimoto SHINOHARA and SAIGO's younger brother, Kobe.

The battle of Tabaru Slope continued for seventeen days in the rain, and the Satsuma army, which was on the backfoot, had no choice but to flee to Yatsushiro, Hitoyoshi, Miyazaki and Nobeoka.

The Satsuma army, which went up north to Nobeoka, tried to take up the positions centering on Wada Pass to

make a counterattack, but it had been already surrounded by the government army. SAIGO, who entrusted the commands of military units to each commander, declared an order of dissolution to his whole army:

[Now our troops got into extremely critical situation. On this occasion, those who want to surrender should do so, and those who want to die should do so.
It is up to you what to do.]

After this declaration, all the soldiers cried, and 4,000 soldiers regretfully surrendered to the government forces. The remaining soldiers numbered only 500.

They looked as if a pack of tigers and leopards were heading for their home.

SAIGO asked Kumakichi to tell Aikana's son, Kikujiro, who had got shot at his right leg at Kumamoto Castle, but still followed his father (SAIGO), to surrender afterwards, and have medical treatment.

And then, SAIGO burned the army general's undress uniform and important papers in the garden of Kodama's residence, where the Headquarters of SAIGO's army was placed.

He said good-bye to his two dogs, which he had brought with him, and freed them. SAIGO army, which numbered only 500, managed to escape from Mt. Eno surrounded by the government troops, and arrive at the summit through the trackless, rugged surface of Mt. Eno. Avoiding the government's attack on the way, they were heading for Kagoshima by helping each other, walking heavily through mountains, rivers and valleys. On their way to

Kagoshima, receiving villagers' heartwarming aid and encouraging words, they finally arrived at Yoshida Village in Kagoshima. It happened on September 1. They returned home for the first time in 199 days. The people outside and inside of Kagoshima City who heard the news that SAIGO had returned rejoiced, and their joy welled up at his brilliant feat that he had gone into Kagoshima and occupied Shiroyama. The civilians tried to deliver food, clothes and weapons, but the government forces took all of them away. As a result, only small parts of them were successfully delivered to Shiroyama.

On September, 4, the SAIGO's Drawn Sword Squad, which comprised 70 soldiers, made an assault on the government army's base at Komekura (the vicinity of the present City Office), but they were suppressed after they fought bravely for some time. Among them, there was a commander of the Nakatsu-tai troops, Sotaro MASUDA. When he received an order of dissolution, he said to his members, "You are young, so return home, and work for everybody. I'll follow Mr. SAIGO to the last." Thus, his troops broke up.

Shiroyama was very closely surrounded by the 5,8000 soldiers of the government army. Within the SAIGO's army, they talked about a plea for saving SAGO's life.

On September, 13, Shuichiro KONO and Issuke YAMANODA visited the government army's staff officer, Sumiyoshi KAWAMURA, to beg for SAIGO's life. KAWAMURA said frostily, "It is hopeless now. The government army is planning to make an all-out attack at dawn tomorrow. When you return, tell SAIGO to come to our Headquarters by 5:00 O'clock this afternoon if he

has anything to say to me." YAMANODA gave a detailed account of the meeting to SAIGO, who said decisively, "No need to answer."

On hearing this, all the soldiers made up their mind to risk their lives for SAIGO.

That night at Shiroyama, they had a farewell party, surrounding SAIGO.

They drank and sang together. Some recited poems.

They mutually admired their brave fights as if they forgot two hundred or more days of desperate struggle, which seemed like an ancient battlefield.

In the sky, the harvest moon gave off pale light, breaking through the clouds or disappearing behind them. The melody of 'Kimigayo' (Japanese national anthem by Fenton) that the government army played ceremonially flew all around. Both sides of ally and enemy were reluctant to part from one another. The scene on the eve of the Great War was full of sorrow. By Satsuma domain's request, English Fenton had been instructing the military music band and the Music Department of Imperial Household Ministry. Kimigayo's lyrics was the same with the current national anthem, but its melody was western.

At 3:55 AM of September 24, at the report of three blank shots as a signal, the government army started launching an all-out attack. The government army rushed to Shiroyama from all directions. At last, they came close to its hilltop, and then concentrated ammunition there. Furthermore, they showered bullets upon Iwasakitani where SAIGO's Headquarters was located. SAIGO, who was accompanied by several soldiers, came out of a cave, wearing a tight-sleeved kimono, a short skirt, straw

sandals, and a short sword inside a white waistband, and started walking toward Iwasakitaniguchi. A hail of bullets came flying from every quarter. When he went down around 300m, SAIGO had his shoulder and thigh shot. He could not walk. SAIGO said to Shinsuke BEPPU, "Shindon (Shinsuke's nickname), Shindon, that's enough, here is good" And then he dropped to his knees, straightened up, and joined his hands in prayer. Then he faced the East and prayed silently. "Sir! Please forgive me!", Shinsuke cried, and cut off his mentor, SAIGO's head. All the survivors, who knew that SAIGO had died, ran down under a shower of bullets, and fought bravely. Then they died subsequently to SAIGO's death. At 7:00 o'clock in the morning, the sound of gunshots was not heard anymore. The battle was over. After then, suddenly the sky got dark, and thunders roared. Violent rain and wind washed away the dead soldiers' fresh blood. SAIGO's life full of difficulties ended when he was 49 years old.

Retrospectively, SAIGO started up Meiji government as the head of Councilor six years before and contributed to the establishment and enhancement of army and police to protect the nation and its people under the policy to enrich and strengthen the country.

In Seinan war, however, a slight misunderstanding between SAIGO and a part of bureaucrats, whom he had put his heart into bringing up, divided them into friends and enemies and forced them to fight against one another. SAIGO lost his life.

That was an extremely sad incident. However, SAIGO's lifelong belief-soul of "Revere Heaven, Love People", Honesty, and Courtesy and his great achievements made

by working hard for the nation without self-interest will be surely praised throughout the years together with his name of Takamori SAIGO as a" Revolutionary Hero"

In the former Boshin War, SAIGO's sworn ally Kaishu KATSU, who had negotiated with SAIGO and kept the city of Edo from the disasters of war, recalled his exertion in Seinan War and left the following poem:

Without proving your innocence:
Allow your own dear men to do as they like
You have passed away, SAIGO!

This is the poem which enables us to read through Katsu's and SAIGO's feelings.

Conclusion

This book has described the latter half of Takamori SAIGO's eventful life. The reason why SAIGO is admired as a revolutionary hero is because he destroyed the Edo Shogunate of Japan, which lasted for 264 years, and built a state regime with the emperor at its center. Together with his comrades, he succeeded in accomplishing this great achievement nobody could do until then.

SAIGO's belief in saving the country enabled him to tread the path of right, overcome many difficulties and achieve the Meiji Restoration.

I believe that he always lived with the soul of "Revere Heaven, Love People" as his supreme motto.

We should make every effort to strengthen the bonds of human love and build a world where everybody can live comfortably, thinking of SAIGO's spirit of "Revere Heaven, Love People" and taking lessons from the past.

I hope that this book will prove helpful to its readers.

Lastly, I would like to express my heartful gratitude for "Kokushokankokai Inc." and the persons who contributed to the publication of this book.

March, 2021

Author Tomio SAODA
English Translation Yutaka SAODA

著者紹介　竿田　富夫（さおだ　とみお）

昭和31年　鹿児島大学教育学部卒
平成３年　開聞町立開聞小学校長
平成６年　知名町立知名小学校長
平成８年　和泊町教育長
平成15年　和泊西郷南洲顕彰会長
平成20年　同会名誉会長

訳者紹介　竿田　豊（さおだ　ゆたか）

昭和46年　大阪外語大学外国語科卒業
同年　　　和光証券㈱外国部
昭和51年　東京都立淵江高校英語科教員
昭和60年　東京都教育研究員
昭和61年　文部省高等学校英語教育指導者養成講座受講
昭和62年　東京都教育開発委員
同年　　　文部省高等学校英語担当教員米国
　　　　　ブラウン大学海外派遣研修
平成10年　東京都立向島商業高校教頭
平成13年　東京都立八潮高校教頭
平成16年　東京都立新宿山吹高校副校長
平成19年　定年退職

西郷（せご）どんと維新（いしん）の風（かぜ）――敬天愛人（けいてんあいじん）の始（はじ）まり、沖永良部島（おきのえらぶじま）

2021年４月25日　初版第１刷発行

著　者　竿田富夫
訳　者　竿田豊
発行者　佐藤今朝夫
発行所　株式会社 国書刊行会
〒174-0056 東京都板橋区志村１-13-15
TEL 03 (5970) 7421　FAX 03 (5970) 7427
https://www.kokusho.co.jp

印刷・製本　三松堂株式会社
装　幀　真志田桐子
書籍コーディネート　インプルーブ　小山睦男

ISBN 978-4-336-07199-6